AA

G000043855

Cycle Rides

Lake District
& the Northwest

Publisher: David Watchus
Managing Editor: Isla Love
Senior Editor: Donna Wood
Senior Designer: Kat Mead
Picture Research: Lesley Grayson
Cartographic Editor: Geoff Chapman
Cartographic Production: Anna Thompson

Produced by AA Publishing
© Automobile Association Developments Limited 2007

Published by AA Publishing (a trading name of Automobile Association Developments Limited, whose registered office is Fanum House, Basing View, Basingstoke, Hampshire RG21 4EA; registered number 1878835).

 This product includes mapping data licensed from the Ordnance Survey® with the permission of the Controller of Her Majesty's Stationery Office. © Crown copyright 2007. All rights reserved. Licence number 100021153.

A03033C

ISBN-10: 0-7495-5192-5
ISBN-13: 978-0-7495-5192-6
A CIP catalogue record for this book is available from the British Library.

Visit AA Publishing's website www.theAA.com/travel

Colour reproduction by Keene Group, Andover
Printed in Italy by Canale & C SPA

Cycle Rides

Lake District
& the Northwest

Contents

Locator map

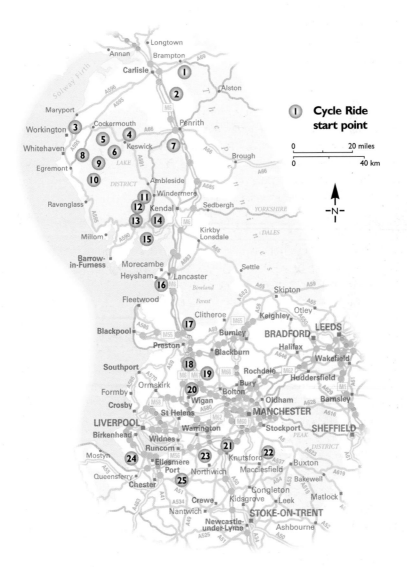

● Longtown
Annan   Brampton
Carlisle   **①**
②   ●Alston
●Maryport
Workington **③** ●Cockermouth   Penrith
⑤   **④**
Whitehaven   **⑥** Keswick   **⑦**
⑧ **⑨**   ●Brough
●Egremont   *LAKE*
⑩   *DISTRICT*   ●Ambleside
●Ravenglass   **⑪** ●Windermere
⑫ Kendal   ●Sedbergh   *YORKSHIRE*
⑬ **⑭**
●Millom   **⑮**   Kirkby *DALES*
Lonsdale
Barrow-
in-Furness   ●Morecambe   ●Settle
Heysham● ●Lancaster
⑯   *Bowland*
●Fleetwood   *Forest*   ●Skipton
Clitheroe   Otley●
⑰   Keighley●   ●LEEDS
●Blackpool   Burnley● **BRADFORD**
Preston● ●Blackburn   Halifax●
Southport   **⑱**   ●Wakefield
⑲ ●Rochdale   ●Huddersfield
●Ormskirk   Bury●
Formby●   **⑳** ●Bolton   Oldham● Barnsley●
●Crosby   Wigan●   ●**MANCHESTER**
●St Helens
LIVERPOOL   ●Warrington   Stockport● **SHEFFIELD**
●Birkenhead   *PEAK*
Widnes● **㉑**
Mostyn● **㉔** Runcorn●   *DISTRICT*
●Ellesmere   **㉓** Knutsford● **㉒** ●Buxton
Queensferry● Port   ●Northwich   ●Macclesfield
㉕   ●Bakewell
●Chester   ●Congleton
A534 ●Crewe Kidsgrove● ●Leek   ●Matlock
Nantwich●
Newcastle-   **STOKE-ON-TRENT**
under-Lyme   ●Ashbourne

① **Cycle Ride**
    start point

0   20 miles
0   40 km

↑
-N-
|

5

Introduction to Lake District & the Northwest

The Lake District and the Northwest of England has long been a favourite region with families looking for a holiday offering beautiful scenery and outdoor activities. As the name suggests, it's full of lakes, which, paradoxically, are not named 'lakes' but rather 'meres' or 'waters', but it is also a place of high sweeping fells; during the 1880s Wasdale Head was identified as the birthplace of rock-climbing. The region is perhaps less well-known as a destination for cycling, but there's plenty of choice, with the designated Coast-to-Coast cycle route, a sculpture trail at Rowrah and trails in Grizedale Forest that offer the chance to see deer and even buzzards. Cycling in the Lake District just wouldn't be the same without following a route by water, so you can circle Ennerdale Water, start a route at England's deepest lake, Wast Water, or pedal alongside England's largest lake, Windermere. In leafy Cheshire, the opportunity to link two of the county's most important country estates, Tatton Park and

trip on Windermere, while a rainy-day option is a visit to Aquarium of the Lakes, on the southern tip of Windermere, or the Lakeland Sheep and Wool Centre. Your cycle ride can have a literary theme if you visit the riverside town of Cockermouth, childhood home of the poet, William Wordsworth, and the Lake District is well-known as Beatrix Potter country. One ride starts from the hamlet of Little Town, the home of Mrs Tiggywinkle, the hedgehog washerwoman. The region has many historic sites which lie near enough to the cycle routes for exploration, such as Castlerigg Stone Circle and Long Meg and Her Daughters at Little Salkeld. Churches range from the tiny whitewashed Newlands Church in Newlands Valley to the church at Cartmel Priory.

The landscape and peace and quiet are the reasons most people come to this region, so this book includes some tranquil routes like the one around Winster Valley. Features of interest include views of the coast and fells from an old railway track at Seaton, Roman remains at Burrow Walls, glimpses of Scafell Pike (England's highest peak) and Crag Fell. The view around the head of Wast Water inspired the National Park logo and could be the best in England.

One factor which may help you choose which route to follow is the nature of the pub we suggest. Indeed, the region is rich with unpretentious pubs, many of which are former coaching inns, housed in centuries-old buildings. The friendly Eagles Head pub on the Grizedale Forest ride says it all with its sign stating 'Walkers and cyclists are always welcome, however muddy'.

Dunham Park, should not be missed, and one cycle ride explores the peaceful Eden Valley, often referred to as the unsung jewel of England due to its unspoilt nature. Of course, the cycle routes do take in some well-known places such as busy Keswick with its wide selection of places to eat and drink. Places to visit before or after your ride include the Beatrix Potter Gallery in Hawkshead and the Lakeland Motor Museum at Holker Hall by Cark. If the weather is fine you can take a steam-yacht

The beautiful view from the shores of Loweswater

Using this book

SHORTER ALTERNATIVE ROUTE

Each cycle ride has a panel giving essential information for the cyclist, including the distance, terrain, nature of the paths, nearest public toilets and cycle hire.

|2| **MAP:** OS Explorer OL24 White Peak

START/FINISH: Rudyard Old Station, grid ref |3| SJ955579

TRAILS/TRACKS: old railway trackbed

LANDSCAPE: wooded lake shore, peaceful pastures and meadows

PUBLIC TOILETS: Rudyard village

|5| **TOURIST INFORMATION:** Leek, tel 01538 483741

|6| **CYCLE HIRE:** none near by

THE PUB: The Abbey Inn, Leek, see 'Directions'

|7| 🛑 Take care along the banks of the lake – keep well away from the shore line

|1| **MINIMUM TIME:** The time stated for completing each ride is the estimated minimum time that a reasonably fit family group of cyclists would take to complete the circuit. This does not allow for rest or refreshment stops.

|2| **MAPS:** Each route is shown on a detailed map. However, some detail is lost because of the restrictions imposed by scale, so for this reason, we recommend that you use the maps in conjunction with a more detailed Ordnance Survey map. The relevant Ordnance Survey Explorer map appropriate for each cycle ride is listed.

|3| **START/FINISH:** Here we indicate the start location and parking area. There is a six-figure grid reference prefixed by two letters showing which 100km square of the National Grid it refers to. You'll find more information on grid references on most Ordnance Survey maps.

|4| **LEVEL OF DIFFICULTY:** The cycle rides have been graded simply (1 to 3) to give an indication of their relative difficulty. Easier routes, such as those with little total ascent, on easy paths or level trails, or those covering shorter distances are graded 1. The hardest routes, either because they include a lot of ascent,

greater distances, or are in hilly, more demanding terrains, are graded 3.

|5| **TOURIST INFORMATION:** The nearest tourist information office and contact number is given for further local information, in particular opening details for the attractions listed in the 'Where to go from here' section.

|6| **CYCLE HIRE:** We list, within reason, the nearest cycle hire shop/centre.

|7| 🛑 Here we highlight any potential difficulties or dangers along the route. At a glance you will know if the route is steep or crosses difficult terrain, or if a cycle ride is hilly, encounters a main road, or whether a mountain bike is essential for the off-road trails. If a particular route is suitable for older, fitter children we say so here.

About the pubs

Generally, all the pubs featured are on the cycle route. Some are located close to the start/finish point, others are at the midway point, and occasionally, the recommended pub is a short drive from the start/finish point. We have included a cross-section of pubs, from homely village locals and isolated rural gems to traditional inns and upmarket country pubs which specialise in food. What they all have in common is that they serve food and welcome children.

The description of the pub is intended to convey its history and character and in the 'food' section we list a selection of dishes, which indicate the style of food available. Under 'family facilities', we say if the pub offers a children's menu or smaller portions of adult dishes, and whether the pub has a family room, high chairs, baby-changing facilities, or toys. There is detail on the garden, terrace, and any play area.

DIRECTIONS: If the pub is very close to the start point we say 'see Getting to the Start'. If the pub is on the route the relevant direction/map location number is given, in addition to general directions. In some cases the pub is a short drive away from the finish point, so we give detailed directions to the pub from the end of the route.

PARKING: The number of parking spaces is given. All but a few of the cycle rides start away from the pub. If the pub car park is the parking/start point, then we have been given permission by the landlord to print the fact. You should always let the landlord or a member of staff know that you are using the car park before setting off.

OPEN: If the pub is open all week we state 'daily' and if it's open throughout the day we say 'all day', otherwise we just give the days/sessions the pub is closed.

FOOD: If the pub serves food all week we state 'daily' and if food is served throughout the day we say 'all day', otherwise we just give the days/sessions when food is not served.

BREWERY/COMPANY: This is the name of the brewery to which the pub is tied or the pub company that owns it. 'Free house' means that the pub is independently owned and run.

REAL ALE: We list the regular real ales available on handpump. 'Guest beers' indicates that the pub rotates beers from a number of microbreweries.

ROOMS: We list the number of bedrooms and how many are en suite. For prices please call the pub.

Please note that pubs change hands frequently and new chefs are employed, so menu details and facilities may change at short notice. Not all the pubs featured in this guide are listed in the *AA Pub Guide*. For information on those that are, including AA-rated accommodation, and for a comprehensive selection of pubs across Britain, please refer to the *AA Pub Guide* or see the AA's website www.theAA.com

Alternative refreshment stops

At a glance you will see if there are other pubs or cafés along the route. If there are no other places on the route, we list the nearest village or town where you can find somewhere else to eat and drink.

☛ Where to go from here

Many of the routes are short and may only take a few hours. You may wish to explore part of the surrounding area after lunch or before tackling the route, so we have selected a few nearby attractions with children in mind.

Cycling in safety

CYCLING

Cycling is a fun activity which children love, and teaching your child to ride a bike and going on family cycling trips are rewarding experiences. Not only is cycling a great way to travel, but as a regular form of exercise it can make an invaluable contribution to a child's health and fitness, and increase their confidence and sense of independence.

However, the growth of motor traffic has made Britain's roads increasingly dangerous and unattractive to cyclists. Cycling with children is an added responsibility and, as with everything, there is a risk when taking them out for a day's cycling. In recent years many measures have been taken to address this, including the on-going development of the National Cycle Network (8,000 miles utilising quiet lanes and traffic-free paths) and local designated off-road routes for families, such as converted railway lines, canal towpaths and forest tracks.

In devising the cycle rides in this guide, every effort has been made to use these designated cycle paths, or to link them with quiet country lanes and waymarked byways and bridleways. Unavoidably, in a few cases, some relatively busy B-roads have been used to link the quieter, more attractive routes.

Rules of the road

- Ride in single file on narrow and busy roads.
- Be alert, look and listen for traffic, especially on narrow lanes and blind bends and be extra careful when descending steep hills, as loose gravel can lead to an accident.
- In wet weather make sure you keep a good distance between you and other riders.
- Make sure you indicate your intentions clearly.
- Brush up on *The Highway Code* before venturing out on to the road.

Off-road safety code of conduct

- Only ride where you know it is legal to do so. It is forbidden to cycle on public footpaths, marked in yellow. The only 'rights of way' open to cyclists are bridleways (blue markers) and unsurfaced tracks, known as byways, which are open to all traffic and waymarked in red.
- Canal towpaths: you need a permit to cycle on some stretches of towpath (www.waterscape.com). Remember that access paths can be steep and slippery and always get off and push your bike under low bridges and by locks.
- Always yield to walkers and horses, giving adequate warning of your approach.
- Don't expect to cycle at high speeds.
- Keep to the main trail to avoid any unnecessary erosion to the area beside the trail and to prevent skidding, especially if it is wet.
- Remember the Country Code.

Cycling with children

Children can use a child seat from the age of eight months, or from the time they can hold themselves upright. There are a number of child seats available which fit on the front or rear of a bike and towable two-seat trailers are worth investigating. 'Trailer bicycles', suitable for five- to ten-year-olds, can be attached to the rear of an adult's bike, so that the adult has control, allowing the child to pedal if he/she wishes. Family cycling can be made easier by using a tandem, as it can carry a child seat and tow trailers. 'Kiddy-cranks' for shorter legs can be fitted to the rear seat tube, enabling either parent to take their child out cycling. With older children it is better to purchase the right size bike rather than one that is too big, as an oversized bike will be difficult to control, and potentially dangerous.

Preparing your bicycle

A basic routine includes checking the wheels for broken spokes or excess play in the bearings, and checking the tyres for punctures, undue wear and the correct tyre pressures. Ensure that the brake blocks are firmly in place and not worn, and that cables are not frayed or too slack. Lubricate hubs, pedals, gear mechanisms and cables. Make sure you have a pump, a bell, a rear rack to carry panniers and, if cycling at night, a set of working lights.

Preparing yourself

Equipping the family with cycling clothing need not be an expensive exercise. Comfort is the key when considering what to wear. Essential items for well-being on a bike are padded cycling shorts, warm stretch leggings (avoid tight-fitting and seamed trousers like jeans or baggy tracksuit trousers that may become caught in the chain), stiff-soled training shoes, and a wind and waterproof jacket. Fingerless gloves will add to your comfort.

A cycling helmet provides essential protection if you fall off your bike, so they

are particularly recommended for young children learning to cycle.

Wrap your child up with several layers in colder weather. Make sure you and those with you are easily visible by car drivers and other road users, by wearing light-coloured or luminous clothing in daylight and reflective strips or sashes in failing light and when it is dark.

What to take with you

Invest in a pair of medium-sized panniers (rucksacks are unwieldy and can affect balance) to carry the necessary gear for you and your family for the day. Take extra clothes with you, the amount depending on the season, and always pack a light wind/waterproof jacket. Carry a basic tool kit (tyre levers, adjustable spanner, a small screwdriver, puncture repair kit, a set of Allen keys) and practical spares, such as an inner tube, a universal brake/gear cable, and a selection of nuts and bolts. Also, always take a pump and a strong lock.

Cycling, especially in hilly terrain and off-road, saps energy, so take enough food and drink for your outing. Always carry plenty of water, especially in hot and humid weather conditions. Consume high-energy snacks like cereal bars, cake or fruits, eating little and often to combat feeling weak and tired. Remember that children get thirsty (and hungry) much more quickly than adults so always have food and diluted juices available for them.

And finally, the most important advice of all—enjoy yourselves!

Talkin Tarn and the end of the Pennines

A varied lane circuit from Talkin Tarn with some expansive views.

Talkin Tarn

Talkin Tarn appears to sit on a shelf on the hillside rather than in a valley. It is around 0.5 mile (800m) long, and big enough to be of value to rowers and scullers, as well as attracting a variety of waders and wildfowl. There is a legend that a drowned village lies at the bottom of the lake, still visible beneath the water. According to local lore, it is the village of Brampton, drowned in a great storm after its inhabitants refused hospitality to a weary traveller. However, divers have found little to support the tale.

The small parking area after the main climb has a couple of benches well placed to enjoy the view. This extends out over the lowlands that run west to the city of Carlisle, with the Solway Firth beyond. All along the northern skyline are the rolling hills of the Scottish Borders. Looking back over your left shoulder there's also a fine view of the Lakeland hills, with Helvellyn, Blencathra and Skiddaw all in the frame. A pebble mosaic representing the view over Talkin Tarn sits prettily in the foreground.

the ride

1 From the **car park** roll back down the access lane to the road and turn left, up past the **golf club** entrance, then fork left, signed to Talkin. The surroundings soon open out, with views to the **Pennines** ahead and **Talkin Tarn** down on the left. Follow the lane past **Tarn End House Hotel**, beside the golf course, then descend into a

Above: Looking across fields to Talkin Tarn and the Scottish hills beyond

The level crossing at Bramptonfell Gates

| 1h00 | 6.75 MILES | 10.9 KM | LEVEL 1 2 3 |

small valley and climb out the other side, with one fairly steep section, into **Talkin village**. Pass the **Hare and Hounds** pub on the right to reach a junction, with the **Blacksmiths Arms** ahead.

2 Turn left on a road that's level, then descend slightly to a junction. Go right, signed to Hallbankgate. The lane climbs steadily, with a short steep section just past the rhyming **Hullerbank** and **Ullerbank**. The reward for this effort is the great view that opens up as the road levels out. The best place to enjoy this is just after another road comes in from the right, where there's a small parking area – but beware of the loose gravel.

3 Continue along the lane, enjoying level progress, with more chances to enjoy the panorama, and also the view up to the rolling moorland slopes on the right. Keep straight on past another road joining from the left; the road still runs more or less level, with only minor undulations, for about 1 mile (1.6km).

4 Not too far into the descent make a sharp left turn at **Cleugh Head**. Cycle past a pretty row of cottages and then head into a fairly steep, twisting descent through shady **woods**. The woods open out into farmland and the gradient eases before **Kirkhouse**. Keep left here at a junction with a triangle of grass. In a little over 0.5 mile (800m), the lane runs beside **plantations** on the right.

5 Look for a rough lane, appearing more of a track, with grass down the middle, bearing off to the right just before a slight rise. This is completely unsigned but it is

MAP: OS Explorer 315 Carlisle

START/FINISH: car park at Talkin Tarn Country Park; grid ref: NY544591

TRAILS/TRACKS: lanes, one short, slightly rougher section

LANDSCAPE: wooded farmland rising to fringes of high moorland

PUBLIC TOILETS: behind the tea room at Talkin Tarn

TOURIST INFORMATION: Brampton, tel 016977 3433

CYCLE HIRE: Scotby Cycles, Carlisle, tel 01228 546931

THE PUB: Blacksmiths Arms, Talkin Village, see Point **2** on route

🚸 The ups and down are not severe and there's a short section of rough lane. Suitability: children 7+

Getting to the start

Talkin Tarn Country Park lies 2 miles (3.2km) south east of Brampton. It is signposted from the B6413, on a lane just south of a level crossing, with a car park and tea room.

Why do this cycle ride?

From Talkin Tarn this route climbs steadily through Talkin village and on to the edge of high moors which are almost the last gasp of the Pennines. A level promenade along the heights gives huge views on a clear day. This is followed by an enjoyable descent, more pleasant lanes and an old-style level crossing just before the finish.

Researched and written by: Jon Sparks

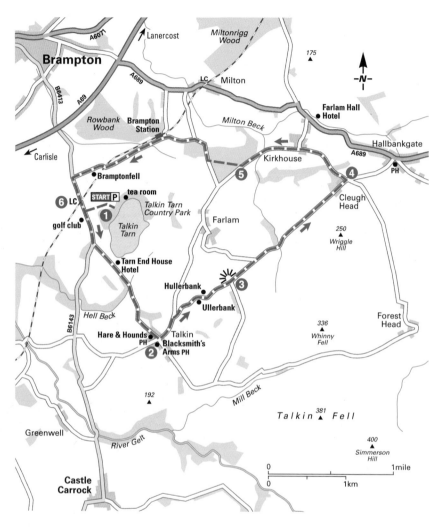

a public road. Follow this down, bumpy but with no real difficulties, until at the end it drops more steeply to a T-junction back on to real tarmac. Turn right and descend a bit more, then go up and round a bend to another junction. Go left, signed to Brampton Junction. Continue down a bit further, past a small pool in the trees on the left, to reach **Brampton Station**. Continue beside the railway. The lane eventually pulls away and rises slightly,

then swings back right to cross a bridge over the line. Keep on past the large farm of **Bramptonfell** to a T-junction and back on to the **B6413**. Turn left, and in 300yds (274m) reach the level crossing at **Bramptonfell Gates**.

6 If the gates are open, cross and continue up the road another 200yds (183m), and turn left back onto the access lane to **Talkin Tarn** and the **car park**.

Blacksmiths Arms

The 18th-century Blacksmiths Arms was originally the local smithy. Today it is all you would expect of a traditional inn: whitewashed walls without, and low-beamed ceilings, horse-brasses, plain wooden tables and local Jennings beer within the rambling small bars. Add a genuinely friendly welcome, clean and comfortable bedrooms and good value home-cooked food and you have a super base from which to explore Hadrian's Wall, the Scottish Borders and the Lake District. There's also a sheltered garden to the rear, plus a few tables at the front overlooking the village green.

Food
The well-balanced menu and blackboard specials offer a good variety of dishes, including lunchtime snacks and traditional Sunday roasts. Using meats and vegetables supplied by local farms, options include sweet-and-sour chicken, Cumberland sausage, beef lasagne, fresh haddock fillet, a vegetarian bake, venison casserole, and duck breast in orange sauce.

Family facilities
Children are welcome inside, and younger family members have their own menu to choose from.

Alternative refreshment stops
Tea room at Talkin Tarn Country Park, the Hare and Hounds in Talkin village, pubs and cafés in nearby Brampton.

about the pub

Blacksmiths Arms
Talkin Village, Brampton
Cumbria CA8 1LE
Tel 016977 3452
www.blacksmithsarmstalkin.co.uk

DIRECTIONS: on the south side of the main junction in the village
PARKING: 6 (use village lane)
OPEN: daily
FOOD: daily
BREWERY/COMPANY: free house
REAL ALE: Hawk's Head, Jennings Cumberland Ale, guest ales
ROOMS: 8 en suite

☛ Where to go from here
Lanercost Priory is an atmospheric 12th-century ruined abbey, north east of Brampton and close to Hadrian's Wall (www.lanercost.co.uk).

The Eden Valley from Armathwaite

Discover an unsung but lovely Cumbrian corner, with exciting off-road options.

The Eden Valley
This route offers great views of both the Lake District and the Pennines, the latter being particularly well seen on the final descent. The highest peak is Cross Fell. At 2,930ft (893m) it is the highest peak in the Pennines and indeed the highest in England outside the Lake District, but it is merely part of a massive mountain wall that hems in the Eden Valley to the east. It has a major influence on local weather and has its very own wind, the notorious Helm wind, possibly so called because it is accompanied by a helmet-like cap of cloud on the ridge.

The railway line which is crossed several times on the right – at track level if you take the first off-road option – is the Settle to Carlisle line, one of Britain's most scenic rail routes. It runs for 72 miles (116km) between Settle in North Yorkshire and Carlisle. Completed in 1876, the line was a major engineering challenge, with 20 viaducts and 14 tunnels. Its highest point is at Ais Gill summit, 1,169ft (356m) above sea level, and its most famous feature is probably the great Ribblehead viaduct, a few miles further south. It was the expense of restoring this, as well as general maintenance of the route, that led to a threat of closure in the 1990s, but a vigorous public campaign and the promotion of the line as a tourist attraction ensured its survival.

Top right: Railway viaduct near Armathwaite
Right: A cyclist using an unmanned crossing over the Settle to Carlisle rail line

the ride

1 Head north through the village and past the church, ignoring all turnings to right and left. Continue along this lane, with a few minor undulations before a dip alongside a railway viaduct. Now climb, in two stages, to the level crossing at **Lowhouse Crossing**. Bump across the line and continue less steeply to a junction near **Froddle Crook**. The old, rusty signpost has lost one arm.

2 For the shorter ride, turn left here and follow the lane beside **High Stand Plantation**, with fine views, to the crossroads at **Blackmoss Pool**. Go straight across to rejoin the longer route. For the longer route, go straight ahead at Froddle Crook for 1.5 miles (2.4km) to a turning on the left signed to Cotehill.

3 To stay on tarmac turn left here and follow the road for 1 mile (1.6km) to the crossroads in **Cotehill village**, then turn left. For the off-road alternative, continue straight ahead to a bridge over the railway

and then past a small **wood** on the left. At the end of the wood follow a bridleway sign left through a gate and down a short track. Where this bends left into a farmyard go straight ahead, through an awkward gate, and follow field edges, with no real track but no great difficulty unless the grass is high. At the bottom of the second field, just below the railway line, bear right on a short track to a gate and out onto the tracks. Cross with care – there is good visibility both ways. Go through the gate on the other side and straight out along a green track, rounding a bend to reach a clearer track. Follow this more easily, to emerge onto a road. Turn left for a short climb into **Cotehill**. Be alert where the road squeezes between two houses. At a crossroads, go straight across to rejoin the road alternative.

4 Carry straight on, signposted to Armathwaite. Climb to **Stand End**, then on beside **High Stand Plantation** to the crossroads at **Blackmoss Pool** (more marsh than open water).

5 Turn right, signed to Aiketgate and Low Hesket. The tree-lined lane runs dead straight, first down, then up. A view of the fells opens up as the road dips to a T-junction. Turn left, signed to Nunclose and Armathwaite, and make a short climb into the hamlet of **Aiketgate**. A fork in the road, opposite the phone box, offers another off-road option.

6 To stay on tarmac, keep right here, and then bear left at the next fork. The lane begins a fine sweeping descent and the off-road alternative rejoins halfway down,

1h30	10 MILES	16.1 KM	LEVEL 1 2 3

LONGER ROUTE (OFF ROAD)

2h00	11 MILES	17.7 KM	LEVEL 1 2 3

SHORTER ALTERNATIVE ROUTE

1h00	6.5 MILES	10.4 KM	LEVEL 1 2 3

MAP: OS Explorer OL5 The English Lakes (NE) and OL315 Carlisle

START/FINISH: Armathwaite village; grid ref: NY504461

TRAILS/TRACKS: lanes, with two optional off-road sections

LANDSCAPE: rolling farmland, woodland and river valley, views to distant fells

PUBLIC TOILETS: none on route

TOURIST INFORMATION: Carlisle, tel: 01228 625600

CYCLE HIRE: Scotby Cycles, Carlisle, tel 01228 546931

THE PUB: The Duke's Head, Armathwaite

❶ Crosses rail tracks twice. The shorter road route is suitable for children 8+; the longer loop is for children 10+. Two optional off-road sections: the first is suitable for most abilities, the second is rougher and steeper, for experienced children 12+ only, mountain bike recommended

Getting to the start

Armathwaite east of Low Heskett and High Heskett, off the A6. There is no car park, so park considerately on verges.

Why do this cycle ride?

One of the unsung jewels of England, the Eden Valley retains a peaceful atmosphere that can be missing in the Lake District.

Researched and written by: Jon Sparks

at **Windy Nook**. For the off-road adventure, take the left fork at Point 6. The tarmac lane leads into a stonier track, climbing steeply at first. The gradient eases, but the track continues stony all the way to the crest. The descent ahead is on a much greener track. This isn't difficult, just a little bumpy, but in summer the vegetation makes it hard to see where your wheels are going. Go through a gate and continue downhill, gradually curving right. The undergrowth

diminishes as the descent steepens. The final 100yds (91m) before the road are steep and tricky, with large stones and no soft landings: consider walking here. Rejoin the road at **Windy Nook** and turn left.

Continue on this road past the turning for Nunclose. The road swings round towards another railway viaduct. Keep left at another junction, go under the railway, and follow the road back into **Armathwaite**.

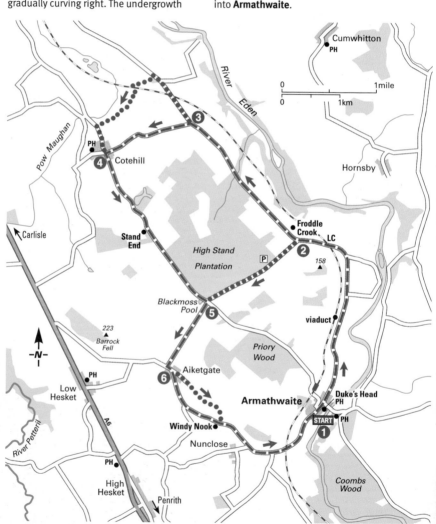

The Duke's Head

about the pub

The Duke's Head
Armathwaite, Carlisle
Cumbria CA4 9PB
Tel 016974 72226

DIRECTIONS: From the A6 take the Armathwaite turning
PARKING: 40
OPEN: daily, all day
FOOD: daily
BREWERY/COMPANY: Punch Taverns
REAL ALE: Black Sheep, guest ales
ROOMS: 5 bedrooms (3 en suite)

A long-standing favourite in the area, the comfortable, stone-built Duke's Head stays firmly traditional. Its fishing connections are well documented in the Last Cast Lounge, from where it's only a few paces into a glorious garden with flower beds and beech trees disappearing down the banks of the River Eden below. Fishing can be arranged for guests, who come here in search of the finest trout and salmon in the north of England. Expect stone walls, open log fires, oak tables and settles in the civilised lounge bar, a lively locals' bar dispensing tip-top bitter, and simply furnished bedrooms. The inn's bold claim to be the 'home of probably the best roast duck in Cumbria' is one which many will feel obliged to put to the test. Cyclists exploring the valley are made very welcome, and the pub even has some bikes for hire.

Food

Fresh local produce features on the wide-ranging menu. If you don't fancy roast duck, try hot potted Solway shrimps, venison steak with red wine, mushroom and redcurrant sauce, locally smoked salmon or prime steaks from a local farm. Or there are sandwiches and a 3-cheese platter.

Family facilities

Small portions from the main menu are available to children, who are welcome inside the pub. It's a super garden for summer alfresco eating and drinking, but beware of the river.

Alternative refreshment stops

None on route but you'll also find the Fox and Pheasant by the river in Armathwaite.

☞ Where to go from here

Long Meg and Her Daughters is a Bronze Age stone circle at Little Salkeld, south of Kirkoswald (open access).

Eden Valley CUMBRIA

Sea views from the Seaton Track

An easy ride along a former railway with stunning views over coast and fells.

Coast-to-coast route

Several other routes in this book share sections of the C2C (Coast-to-Coast) cycle route, but this one overlooks the start, at the end of a promontory which can be seen beyond Workington harbour. It's traditional for riders to dip their feet (or their wheels) in the sea at each end – this is easier when the tide is in! There's an alternative start to the C2C in Whitehaven, and the two branches meet near Keswick. There are also alternative finishes on the east coast, either at Tynemouth or Sunderland. The full route is around 140 miles (225km) and the record time is under nine hours, though most people take three or four days and some make a much more leisurely passage.

The Roman remains at Burrow Walls were part of a fort that formed a line of sea defences, possibly extending as far south as Ravenglass. This is sometimes considered to be an extension of Hadrian's Wall. Nearby Siddick Pond, a nature reserve, is an important area of wetland habitat consisting of meres and reed beds. It is very close to a large paper mill, which has managed to clean up its emissions substantially in recent years, encouraging wildlife to flourish.

the ride

1 From the parking area outside the **post office** follow a surfaced path left and up to the level of the old railway. Continue, away from the bridges. As you pass under a bridge on the outskirts of Seaton, the views begin to open up. The landscape still has its industrial element, but there is also the Irish Sea and Solway Firth, with the Galloway hills beyond on a clear day. As the route begins to curve to the left under another bridge, you'll glimpse the rooftops of **Workington**. Just beyond this, some rough walls in the field on the left are the remains of **Burrow Walls** Roman fort.

Top: Roman remains at Burrow Walls, Seaton
Left: Bridge at Seaton, with decorated barriers

1h00 **6.75 MILES** **10.9 KM** **LEVEL 123**

MAP: OS Explorer 303 Whitehaven and Workington

START/FINISH: Seaton town centre; grid ref: NY017307

TRAILS/TRACKS: old railway track with tarmac surface; optional return on minor lanes with some grass and stony tracks

LANDSCAPE: farmland with sea and fell views, some industrial landscape

PUBLIC TOILETS: none on route

TOURIST INFORMATION: Workington, tel 01900 606699

CYCLE HIRE: Keswick Mountain Bikes, Keswick, tel 017687 75202

THE PUB: The Coachman Inn, Seaton, near start of route

❗ The railway path is suitable for children of all ages. On the return road loop there are two steep climbs and one steep descent, suitable for more experienced family groups; children 10+

Getting to the start

Seaton is a village 2 miles (3.2km) north of Workington. Approaching from Workington, the main road swings left then dips towards a railway bridge decorated with cycling figures. Turn left before the bridge, at a sign 'Library'. Park in the spaces on the right, outside the post office, or on the street.

Why do this cycle ride?

There's plenty to engage the interest on this simple ride along a well-surfaced old railway, be it fine views over the sea in one direction and the Lakeland Fells in the other, or the remains of the Roman fort at Burrow Walls and a rich variety of wayside flowers.

Researched and written by: Jon Sparks

On the right is **Siddick Pond**, with wind turbines beyond. You soon reach a track junction with a **C2C sign**.

2 Branch down to the right for a closer look at Siddick Pond, then return to the junction and keep straight on. The route winds through a broad cutting then runs out onto a green-railed bridge over the **A596** on the outskirts of Workington. At the further end of the bridge is the **Hagworm Wiggle Path**.

3 For an easy and entirely off-road path, turn round here and retrace the route to **Seaton**. To extend this shorter ride, continue over the bridge and along the railway track for another 2 miles (3.2km) to Point 5. For the alternative, more challenging return loop from Point 3, roll down towards the bridge over the **River Derwent**. Just before reaching it bear left. Cross a grassy area and follow an emerging track bearing left into a new **underpass** below the main road. This leads out to a lane.

4 Continue in the same general direction, initially running parallel to the river. Continue along the narrow surfaced lane, ignoring various gravel tracks branching off. After a **row of cottages** the lane becomes rougher. Keep right at a fork, down to the river.

5 Turn left (upstream). Bump through the cobbled yard at **Seaton Mill** then swing left over a small bridge and bear right at a **Cumbria Cycleway sign**. A stiff climb leads to a T-junction on the outskirts of Seaton. Turn right, back on tarmac. Emerge onto a junction with a grassy island, in front of the **Packhorse pub,** and turn right. Follow the lane, climbing gently, with fine views of the Lakeland Fells. The lane levels off and then dips slightly at a gravel lay-by. The railway track is close by on the left and runs parallel for the next 0.5 mile (800m), but save this for the return as the lane gives better views.

The lane begins to descend – take care as the descent becomes steep and twisting as it drops into **Camerton** village. Keep left past the **Black Lion pub** and change quickly down through the gears as the road climbs steeply out of the village, peaking as it reaches a railway bridge.

6 Immediately before the bridge there's a **cycleway sign** on the left. Negotiate the wiggle barrier and follow the narrow path as it drops down to the railway track at a short section of 'dual carriageway'. The left branch keeps the views for a few yards but they soon rejoin. Continue level and then gently downhill, through a tree-lined cutting and then under a bridge with another wrought-iron wiggle. Pass some railings, then cross the bridges in the centre of **Seaton** village. Make a sharp left turn to drop back down the path to return to the start point in the **post office car park**.

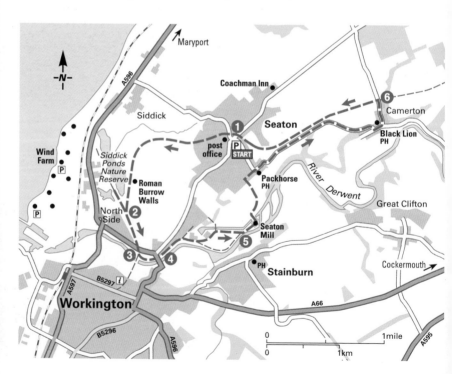

The Coachman Inn

about the pub

The Coachman Inn
43 High Seaton, Seaton
Workington, Cumbria CA14 1LJ
Tel 01900 603976

DIRECTIONS: on the north eastern edge of Seaton	
PARKING: 30	
OPEN: closed Tuesday	
FOOD: daily	
BREWERY/COMPANY: Scottish & Newcastle	
REAL ALE: none available	

It isn't recommended to cycle the 0.5 mile (800m) to The Coachman if you have younger children in tow. The road is relatively busy and it's uphill all the way. Whether you arrive on two wheels or four, the pub is friendly, unpretentious, and well used to cyclists, being close to both the Coast-to-Coast route and the Cumbria Cycleway. Hearty appetites are therefore well catered for with an extensive and reasonably priced menu that includes all the usual pub favourites and a good number of vegetarian options. The beer garden is tucked away at the rear, well away from the road, though this means it doesn't get the views that the pub's elevated position promises.

Food

Main menu dishes include home-made steak pie, lasagne, farmhouse grill, scampi and chips, and vegetarian dishes such as Stilton and vegetable crumble. Look to the specials board for hot and cold baguettes – Cumberland sausage and fried onions. Separate sandwich menu.

Family facilities

The Coachman is a friendly family pub offering a warm welcome to children, a children's menu and a good beer garden.

Alternative refreshment stops

Pubs and cafés in Seaton town centre; on the route you'll find the Packhorse at Low Seaton and the Black Lion in Camerton.

☛ Where to go from here

Maryport's Maritime Museum tells the story of the town's maritime tradition (www.lakedistrict-coastaquarium. co.uk). Alternatively, pay a visit to The Senhouse Roman Museum which contains an impressive collection of Roman artefacts dug from the former fort next door.

From Keswick to Threlkeld

A linear ride along an old railway, with an optional return via Lakeland's greatest ancient site.

The Greta Valley

The railway to Keswick was completed in 1864, having taken just 18 months to build, at a total cost of £267,000 for 31 miles (50km), and with 135 bridges. Goods traffic declined quite early in its life. Passenger numbers peaked in 1913 at 182,000, but never really recovered after World War I, though the line struggled on until it finally closed in 1972.

The railway route passes the bobbin mill site at Low Briery. The Lake District once produced half of all the wooden

Castlerigg Stone Circle in winter

bobbins used by the world's textile industry, and Low Briery alone exported 40 million of these every year.

Whether you cycle there, drive there or take the bus, Castlerigg Stone Circle is a 'must-see' site. It may not be the most impressive such circle in Britain, but it's hard to think of one that has a finer location. Best of all, come early in the morning or late in the evening when there are few others around and your imagination can have free rein. It was probably built around 3000 BC, and no one today knows exactly what it was for, although significant astronomical alignments have been identified.

the ride

1 Ride down towards the **Leisure Centre** and bear left, signed Keswick Railway Footpath, past the former railway station, now a smart hotel. The old trackbed leads

1h30	9 MILES	14.5 KM	LEVEL 1 2 3

SHORTER ALTERNATIVE ROUTE

1h00	8 MILES	12.9 KM	LEVEL 1 2 3

MAP: OS Explorer OL 4 The English Lakes (NW) and OL 5 The English Lakes (NE)

START/FINISH: Keswick Leisure Centre; grid ref: NY269238

TRAILS/TRACKS: old railway track, short section of cycle track beside main road, minor road; optional return on minor roads with short section of busy A road (or walk down pavement alongside)

LANDSCAPE: woodland and river valley; open farmland with views to fells on return via stone circle

PUBLIC TOILETS: Keswick

TOURIST INFORMATION: Keswick, tel 017687 72645

CYCLE HIRE: Keswick Mountain Bikes, Keswick, tel 017687 75202

THE PUB: Horse & Farrier Inn, Threlkeld, see Point **3** on route

❶ Railway path section suitable for all ages. If continuing into Threlkeld, suitability: children 6+; if returning via stone circle, suitability: children 10+

Getting to the start
Follow the A66 to a roundabout north west of Keswick. Take the A5271 towards the town. After 300yds (274m) turn left , signposted 'Leisure Pool' and roadside parking.

Why do this cycle ride?
This route crosses and recrosses the river, running through woodland. Return the same way take the climb to Castlerigg Stone Circle.

Researched and written by: Jon Sparks

on to a bridge over the river and then over the **A5271**. Pass a housing estate on the left, then climb – more steeply than you'd expect from a railway track (the route here was disrupted by the construction of the A66 bypass and bridge). There's a **National Cycle Network/C2C sign** just before the route goes under **Greta Bridge**. At the end of an unusual elevated boardwalk section, look right and you can just see the top of a stone arch, once the mouth of a tunnel, indicating the original line of the railway. Continue with views of the river then past the caravans of **Low Briery**. Go under a bridge and pass an information board about the former **bobbin mill**.

2 Continue across a bridge over the **River Greta**, seemingly a simple flat span but actually supported by an inverted ironwork arch. There's a second, similar bridge, and then a third with its arch 'right side up'. Just before the fourth bridge an **old railway hut** is now a shelter and information point. The bridge overlooks the junction of the river with **Glenderaterra Beck**. Cross another inverted bridge, then go through a short **tunnel** (no need for lights). There's another bridge, another information shelter and then a cutting. Cross another bridge and make a short climb, where the original line of the railway has again been obliterated by the **A66**. Emerge alongside the busy road on a separate cycle track. After about 200yds (183m) swing left on the minor road to **Threlkeld**, and follow it into the village, past the church, to the **Horse & Farrier**.

3 Retrace the route as far as the last bridge you crossed, and go over. (You can, of course, return all the way along the railway track from this point.)

4 About 30yds (27m) past the bridge, turn sharp left through a small gate. A steep

drop down and a bumpy path take you under the A66 and soon lead out to a road. Turn right and climb, with good views of **St John's in the Vale** and **Helvellyn**. Make a sweeping descent and turn left just before it levels out.

5 Swing round through a little valley, then turn left again and climb steadily, now looking down the **Naddle Valley**. The climb is quite long, levelling out just as the **stone circle** appears in a field on the left. Almost at once the road sweeps down again. Drop down to a T-junction on the outskirts of **Keswick**.

6 Families may feel safer walking the next short section. Follow the road left to another T-junction, then turn right down the hill. Round the first bend and just before a **bridge** with slate parapets go left round a barrier onto a gravel path leading down onto the **railway track** and so back to the start.

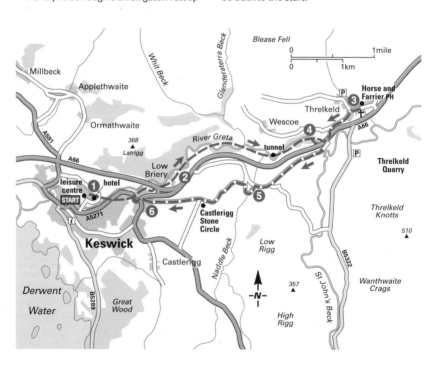

Horse & Farrier Inn

For over 300 years this stone inn has stood in an idyllic position below Blencathra. Ever popular with fell walkers, it provides imaginative home cooking, and real ales from the host brewer, Jennings. It has recently been refurbished, but original features have been retained and restored to their former glory, including slate floors, some fine panelling and oak beams. Hunting prints hang on the walls and warming log fires burn in the grate to create a cosy, welcoming atmosphere. It is noted locally for imaginative, rather restaurant food, although there is plenty of space for drinkers, and walkers are welcome in the bar. Garden seating has views up to the scarred face of Blencathra.

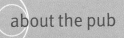

about the pub

Horse & Farrier Inn
Threlkeld, Keswick
Cumbria CA12 4SQ
Tel 01687 79688
www.horseandfarrier.com

DIRECTIONS: on the village main street, east of the church

PARKING: 60

OPEN: daily, all day

FOOD: daily, all day

BREWERY/COMPANY: Jennings Brewery

REAL ALE: Jennings Bitter, Cocker Hoop and Sneck Lifter, Cumberland ale, guest beer

ROOMS: 9 en suite, + self-catering cottage

Food

An adventurous menu offers plenty of choice including fresh fish and local produce. Starters like stir-fried king prawns or smoked haddock and seafood terrine might precede pan-fried venison steak in a juniper marinade or poached sea bass on a bed of risotto with pancetta and wild mushrooms. There's a home-made curry of the day and additional lunchtime fare includes cold and hot open sandwiches, and seasonal salads.

Family facilities

Children are welcome in the bars and overnight. The children's menu offers a standard selection of children's meals, and various puzzles and drawings to colour in.

Alternative refreshment stops

Excellent choice of pubs, cafés and restaurants in Keswick and the Salutation pub in Threlkeld.

☞ Where to go from here

The Cars of the Stars Motor Museum in Keswick houses an unusual collection of cars from film and TV, including Chitty Chitty Bang Bang, the Batmobile and the James Bond cars. North of Keswick on the A591 is Mirehouse, a 17th-century house in a spectacular lakeside setting, near where Tennyson wrote much of *Morte d'Arthur*.

High around Loweswater Fell

⑤

Low Lorton **CUMBRIA**

·A circuit from Low Lorton to Loweswater and back through Lorton Vale.

Alien invaders

Signs on this route draw attention to the peril of red squirrels in the area. The red squirrel is native to Britain but over the last century or so has been widely displaced by the grey squirrel, introduced from North America. Red squirrels have longer bodies and tails than the greys but a much more slender build and are considerably lighter. Today there are an estimated 2.5 million greys to just 160,000 reds, and most of those are found in Scotland. Around 30,000 red squirrels survive in England and Wales, mainly in Cumbria and Northumberland.

The rhododendrons which make such a splash on the fellside above Loweswater are also an introduced species, this time from the Himalayas. Spectacular in bloom, they are tough, hardy mountain plants and

thrive in the acid soils and cool, moist climate of the Lake District. The snag is that, rather like the grey squirrel, they tend to compete all too well with native plant species and if left unchecked can displace native shrubs and flowering plants over large areas. In some areas you may see conservation volunteers working to cut them back – but it is a mammoth task.

the ride

1 Follow the road down to the bridge over the **River Cocker** and round to the right. Shortly after, turn left on a road marked 'Unsuitable for motor vehicles'. This begins to climb almost at once and goes on for about 0.5 mile (800m). The steepest section goes through a tunnel of trees between **Low Bank Farm** and **High Bank**.

View towards Crummock Water from the lane above Thackthwaite

The beautiful view from the shores of Loweswater

2h00 — **9.75 MILES** — **15.7 KM** — **LEVEL 123**

2 Above this the gradient gradually eases. At the same time the surface becomes progressively rougher. This shouldn't pose any problems as long as you keep an eye on the track ahead and pick your moment to look round at the views. And these are great, over **Cockermouth** to the **Solway Firth** and the Galloway hills. There's one more short climb before the lane starts to dip downhill. The descent never gets too steep or too difficult, as long as you keep a good lookout for potholes. This run down levels out over tiny **Catgill Bridge** and brings you to a T-junction onto a road.

3 Turn left and wind past the fine buildings of **Mosser Mains**, just beyond which the road forks. Take the left branch, which climbs gradually up the valley of **Mosser Beck**. There's a steeper section just before **Mossergate Farm**. Once past High Mossergate, the surface again gets rougher as the gradient eases. As the track levels out, the high Lakeland fells begin to appear ahead. Pass the narrow **Graythwaite Wood** (mostly rhododendrons, giving an outlandish splash of colour in early summer) at the start of another swooping descent.

4 The track swings left, traversing a steep hillside above **Loweswater**. The surface is generally better on the steepest part of the descent, although there are still a few potholes. Continue along a rougher section, at a gentler gradient, through a **plantation** and finally down to meet the road just above the lake.

MAP: OS Explorer OL 4 The English Lakes (NW)

START/FINISH: outskirts of Low Lorton; grid ref: NY1532577

TRAILS/TRACKS: quiet lanes, moderately rough tracks with some potholes

LANDSCAPE: woodland, waterside, gentle valley, rough grazing land and moorland

PUBLIC TOILETS: none on route

TOURIST INFORMATION: Cockermouth, tel 01900 822634

CYCLE HIRE: Keswick Mountain Bikes, tel 017687 75202; Grin Up North, Cockermouth, tel 01900 829600

THE PUB: Wheatsheaf Inn, Low Lorton, see Point **1** on route

🛈 One very steep climb. Lengthy off-road descents, but not too difficult. Suitability: children 11+

Getting to the start
Low Lorton lies between Cockermouth and Keswick, off the B5292. Park on wide verges near a phone-box on the B5289, just south of Lorton Hall.

Why do this cycle ride?
This ride has its challenges, including a tough climb early on, but you are repaid. There are fine views, first out over the Cumbrian lowlands to the Solway Firth and the hills of Galloway, in Scotland, then over Loweswater and its encircling fells, and finally up into the heart of the Lake District. There is some wonderful traffic-free riding on good tracks, and two exhilarating descents. These are never difficult, but to enjoy them fully you do need confidence in yourself and your bike.

Researched and written by: Jon Sparks

5 Bear left along the road. There's a short climb as the road veers away from the lake, followed by a slight descent and then a more level section. Crest another slight rise and there's a view of **Crummock Water** and the high fells, with **Great Gable** a prominent rounded peak in the distance. Just a short way down the other side is a turning on the left, signposted to Thackthwaite, and also a **C2C sign**.

6 Turn here and follow this narrow lane through the tiny hamlet of **Thackthwaite**, where a sign says, 'Red Squirrels Please drive slowly' (I'm sure they do!). The lane is undulating but predominantly downhill, bringing you gradually down to the valley floor alongside the beck, past the **caravan park** at Whin Fell and on to a T-junction. Turn right over the bridge to return to the start point.

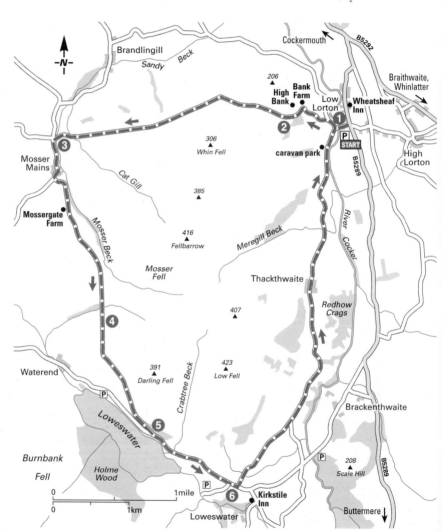

Wheatsheaf Inn

Long, low and white, this 17th-century inn sits squarely along the main road through Low Lorton, just a short way from the start and finish of the ride. The bar, with beams and log fire, is decorated with books and memorabilia to resemble a gamekeeper's lodge. There's another open fire in the non-smoking restaurant. To the rear is a large, safe garden with fine views to the fells, and the pub has a caravan site. There's a selection of beer from the Jennings Brewery in nearby Cockermouth, and good food is a high priority, sourced locally if possible.

Food

A typical menu may include mussels in white wine and garlic sauce or home-made soup to start, followed by beef and beer pie or a half shoulder of lamb served with Cumberland sauce. There are some good fish specials and lighter lunchtime snacks.

Family facilities

Families are welcome inside and there are specific menus for younger children and for teenagers. Extensive rear garden for summer eating and drinking.

about the pub

Wheatsheaf Inn
Low Lorton, Cockermouth
Cumbria CA13 9UW
Tel 01900 85199
www.wheatsheafinnlorton.co.uk

DIRECTIONS: on the B5289, between Low Lorton and Lorton Hall
PARKING: 40
OPEN: daily in summer, closed Monday lunch October to May
FOOD: daily
BREWERY/COMPANY: Jennings Brewery
REAL ALE: Jennings Bitter, Cumberland Ale and seasonal beers

Alternative refreshment stops

Close to Point 6, in Loweswater village, you'll find the Kirkstile Inn (good food and home-brewed beer).

☛ Where to go from here

Wordsworth's childhood home in the riverside town of Cockermouth is well worth a visit. Next door there is a working printing museum, The Printing House, with an interesting range of historic presses and equipment. At the Lakeland Sheep and Wool Centre children can see 19 different breeds of sheep, as well as shearing demonstrations and sheepdog trials. Alternatively, enjoy a tour of the Jennings Brewery.

Low Lorton CUMBRIA

Meandering in Newlands

A classic Lakeland cycle route in Newlands Valley, west of Derwent Water.

Newlands Valley

Tiny Newlands Church is whitewashed on the outside and white painted within, making it a light and airy place as well as one of great peace. It was rebuilt in 1843 on the site of an earlier church, and has a 17th-century pulpit and communion table. It is unusual among English parish churches in having no dedication to a particular saint. It stands close to the hamlet of Little Town, which is said to have inspired children's author Beatrix Potter to set there the story of Mrs Tiggywinkle, the hedgehog washerwoman.

The ride gives great fell views, but glimpses of only one lake – Bassenthwaite, to the north. And here's a good pub quiz question: how many lakes are there in the Lake District? Based on names, the answer is just one – Bassenthwaite Lake. All the rest are 'meres' or 'waters'. Bassenthwaite has recently gained new prominence as the site chosen by the first ospreys to nest in England since 1840. They arrived at Bassenthwaite in 2001, an event that gave the district a huge boost in the wake of the dreadful foot-and-mouth epidemic which devastated the area in that year.

the ride

1 From the parking place head up the steep hill to **Little Town**. Once through Little Town, relax and enjoy a fine winding, mostly downhill, run through the valley to **Stair** and a junction at the bottom of a hill.

2 Turn sharp right on to a narrow lane. The sign, half-hidden by vegetation, says 'Skelgill – Narrow Gated Road'. Climb again, not too steeply, with the hill of **Cat Bells** ahead. The lane steepens as it twists through the tiny hamlet of **Skelgill**, reaching a gate just above. The gate forces a stop,

and it is the top of the climb, so a good place for a look around. To the left of the isolated **Swinside Hill**, to the north, the stretch of water you can see is **Bassenthwaite Lake**. The lane passes a small parking area before reaching a T-junction on a bend. Turn left, downhill, over a cattle-grid and round another sharp bend. There'll usually be lots of parked cars here as it's the start of the main route up Cat Bells. The road levels out, then climbs to a junction.

3 Go left; the junction proves to be triangular. Go left again. As the road swings round to the right there are great views up the valley and the surrounding fells: **Maiden Moor**, **Dale Head**, **Hindscarth** and **Robinson**. Just beyond is the **Swinside Inn**. Turn right beside the pub on a narrow lane signed to Ullock and Braithwaite. Keep left where a road branches off right to Ullock.

4 Cross a stone-arched bridge over **Newlands Beck** and begin a short climb, steep at the start. As it levels out there's another fleeting glimpse of **Bassenthwaite Lake**. At a T-junction turn sharp left. The road runs south, generally level along the base of the steep slopes, and just high enough above the valley floor to give open views. Dip down to a small bridge. Just beyond is the start of the principal walkers' path up **Causey Pike**; you may well see figures struggling up the initial steep slope of **Rowling End**. A little further on, keep straight on past a sharp left turn (for Stair, Portinscale and Grange). For a little while the views are blocked by trees, mostly

Farmhouses in Newlands Vale

1h15 — **7 MILES** — **11.3 KM** — **LEVEL 1 2 3**

MAP: OS Explorer OL 4 The English Lakes (NW)
START/FINISH: near Little Town, south of Skelgill; grid ref: NY232194
TRAILS/TRACKS: lanes, mostly quiet
LANDSCAPE: gentle part-wooded valley surrounded by rugged fells
PUBLIC TOILETS: none on route
TOURIST INFORMATION: Keswick, tel 017687 72645
CYCLE HIRE: Keswick Mountain Bikes, tel 017687 75202; Grin Up North, Cockermouth, tel 01900 829600
THE PUB: Swinside Inn, Newlands, see Point **3** on route
🛈 Some ups and down but not too severe. Suitability: children 8+

Getting to the start
Little Town is a hamlet between Buttermere and Derwent Water, on a narrow lane 4 miles (6.4km) south of Braithwaite. Roadside parking is at the bottom of the hill, just south west of Little Town.

Why do this cycle ride?
Though close to Keswick's bustle, the Newlands valley lacks any major visitor attractions. As a happy result, rather like the Duddon valley in the south, it still feels like the Lake District is supposed to. It's still a place where farming matters as much as fell walking and where visitors can slip back into an easier pace of life. It is also surrounded by scenery that, even by Lakeland standards, is stunning. This is a Lake District cycling route par excellence; of course that means a few hills, but most of the going is easy.

Researched and written by: Jon Sparks

Newlands

CUMBRIA

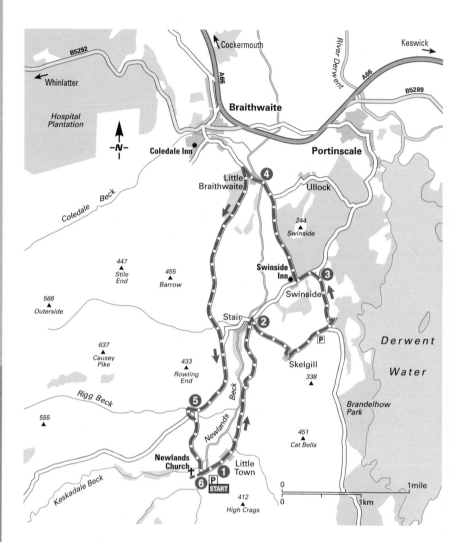

beech and larch, before the classic scene of the dale head begins to open up.

5 Very shortly, a steep stony track drops off to the left to a ford. Those seeking a moment's mountain-bike excitement can choose this track – it merely cuts off a short corner of the road. More sedately, continue round over a bridge to a **wooden house**. Turn left (signed to Newlands Church, Little Town) and drop down, then swing round,

heading straight up the valley with its glorious range of fells ahead.

6 As you come right down into the valley bottom, turn right on the no-through road to **Newlands Church** , which is closer even than the advertised 0.25 mile (400m). Retrace the cycle route to the last junction and turn right, where it's only a few more pedal strokes to reach the bridge and the **car park** just beyond.

Swinside Inn

6

Situated in the peaceful Newlands valley, a world away from the hustle and bustle of Keswick, the Swinside Inn is a listed building dating back to about 1642. From the pub there are stunning views of Causey Pike and Cat Bells – among other landmarks. Although it's been modernised over the years, the two rustic and rambling bars retain many original features, including head-cracking low oak beams, winter log fires and a fine traditional black oak dresser in one of the bars. Good wholesome food, comfortable en suite bedrooms and a patio garden with memorable Lakeland views.

Food

The lunchtime menu is well adapted to hungry cyclists and walkers, with soup, sandwiches, ploughman's and a selection of cooked meals including home-made pies (steak, or chicken, mushroom and sage). The evening menu retains the pies and traditional pub favourites, alongside locally caught trout or Swinside chicken.

Family facilities

Children are welcome in the bars and overnight. There's a children's menu and older children can order small portions of main menu dishes. Safe garden.

about the pub

Swinside Inn
Newlands, Keswick
Cumbria CA12 5UE
Tel 01768778253
www.theswinsideinn.com

DIRECTIONS: 2.25 miles (3.6km) south west of Portinscale on a minor road signed to Newlands
PARKING: 50
OPEN: daily, all day
FOOD: daily
BREWERY/COMPANY: Scottish & Newcastle
REAL ALE: Theakston's Best, Jennings Cumberland Ale, guest beer
ROOMS: 6 en suite

Alternative refreshment stops

None on route. Pubs and cafés in Braithwaite (near Point 4) and in Keswick.

☛ Where to go from here

Whinlatter Forest is England's only true mountain forest. Visit the Osprey viewpoint at Dodd Wood and the Osprey exhibition at Whinlatter (www.ospreywatch.co.uk).

Newlands

CUMBRIA

Around Askham and Bampton

A pleasing loop, rich in ancient hedgerows and fine open scenery.

Fabulous flora

This is a great ride for wildflower-spotting as the low altitude and sunny aspect conspire with the limestone-based soils to produce a wide variety of blooms along the waysides. The lane up the east side of the valley, after Bampton Grange, is particularly rewarding. The hedges along the initial section are full of white hawthorn blossom in May and dog-roses in June. After the main climb on this section there are some fine flowery banks along the lane, with masses of cow parsley and some impressive sweeps of reddish-purple bloody cranesbill, a species of geranium. The name 'cranesbill' comes from the shape of its seed-pods.

A little further on, pause on Crookwath bridge to look down on the streamers of water crowfoot, an aquatic type of buttercup, with white flowers in early summer. Most of the trees along the banks are alder. Alder is happy growing 'with its feet in the water', and the wood it yields is remarkably water-resistant. (The city of Venice is largely built on alderwood piles.)

the ride

1 From the **car park** follow the main road south through the village, dog-legging past the **The Queens Head** pub, with the greens stretching off to left and right. Keep on along this road, enjoying the generally easy gradients and views down the valley ahead to the **Shap Fells**. Across the valley on the left is the sharp profile of **Knipe Scar**.

2 After just over 1 mile (1.6km), on the boundary of **Helton**, branch off right on a loop road through the village. The extra climb is worth it for the pretty cottages and flowery verges. Ease back down to rejoin the valley road and continue, with a network of limestone walls and small fields flanking the road on the right. As the road starts to descend, two lanes branch off to the right from a shared junction.

Fell ponies grazing in fields above Heltondale with Beck and Knipe Scar on the skyline

A limestone wall and dog-rose bush on a lane near Bampton Grange

3 Take the left-hand lane and follow it for 400yds (366m) to a cattle grid, for a look at the **old mill**, with an overgrown watercourse, on **Heltondale Beck**. Continue a little further until the lane reaches open fell. There are good views here and you may sometimes find fell ponies grazing. Retrace to the road at Point 3 and turn right to continue, now descending. At the bottom swing right over **Beckfoot Bridge** and continue along the level valley floor, passing another collection of pretty cottages at **Butterwick**. Note that the walls here have changed from silvery limestone to greyer Lakeland rock. Climb a little before reaching the outskirts of **Bampton**, then go down into the village.

4 The post office and village shop (open long hours) has a café attached, information panels on the wall and more information inside. Over the bridge opposite the shop, it's just a short way up the lane to the pretty **Mardale Inn**. (Those looking for a longer ride could continue up this lane for 2 miles/3.2km to **Naddle Bridge** and **Haweswater**.) Continue along the main valley road towards **Bampton Grange**, swinging left into the village over a bridge crossing the **River Lowther**, and past the **Crown and Mitre** pub.

5 On the edge of the village, turn left, signposted 'Knipe, Whale'. Look back to the left over **Bampton Grange**, with the fells behind rising to the great smooth ridges along which the Romans built their road now known as **High Street**. Cross a

1h15 — **9 MILES** — **14.2 KM** — **LEVEL 1**23

MAP: OS Explorer OL 5 The English Lakes (NE)

START/FINISH: village car park, Askham; grid ref: NY513237

TRAILS/TRACKS: quiet lanes

LANDSCAPE: open valley with pasture and woodland, views to higher fells

PUBLIC TOILETS: none on route

TOURIST INFORMATION: Penrith, tel 01768 867466

CYCLE HIRE: Keswick Mountain Bikes, tel 017687 75202

THE PUB: The Queens Head, Askham, see Point **1** on route

❶ Few steep climbs and descents. Suitability: children 8+

Getting to the start

Askham is south of Penrith and the M6, junction 40. From there, take the A66 east. Turn right on the A6, go through Eamont Bridge, then turn right on the B5320. Go over a railway bridge, then turn left to reach Askham. There is a signposted car park on the left as you enter the village.

Why do this cycle ride?

The valley of the River Lowther runs south from Askham. Delightful on a fine day, it may also escape the worst of the weather when it's raining, as it lies in the 'rain shadow' of the Lakeland fells. This pleasant road circuit has few steep gradients and is away from the main tourist routes.

Researched and written by: Jon Sparks

Askham

CUMBRIA

cattle grid on to open fell. Look up to the right to the low crags of **Knipe Scar**. The lane climbs gently, with great views of the valley and the fells to the west. Descend to a junction by a **phone box** and turn right through a gate. Climb quite steeply to another gate, beyond which the road continues to climb more gradually. The going levels off for a stretch before beginning to descend. Whizz back down into the valley, keeping straight on at a junction, and down to the river at **Crookwath Bridge**.

6 The climb away from the river is gentle but quite sustained, levelling off just before a T-junction. Emerge with care as some traffic moves quite fast here, and go right, almost immediately back into **Askham**.

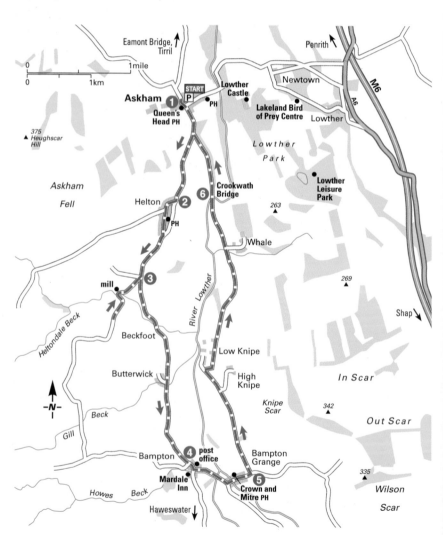

The Queens Head

7

A picture-book village complete with river, church and castle is the lovely setting for this popular late 17th-century pub. Lowther Castle is just a few minutes' walk away. The bar has low ceilings, horse-brasses, copper kettles and some stuffed animal heads, but the best features are the old fireplace (dated 1682) and the wall cupboard alongside, dated 1698. There is also a rambling, beamed lounge, roaring log fires and a games room with pool and darts. Outdoor seating is limited to two small paved areas, and the front benches overlook the village green.

about the pub

The Queens Head
Askham, Penrith
Cumbria CA10 8PF
Tel 01931 712225

DIRECTIONS: in the centre of Askham, near Lowther Castle	
PARKING: 8 (village car park adjacent)	
OPEN: daily, all day in summer	
FOOD: daily	
BREWERY/COMPANY: Vaux Brewery	
REAL ALE: Tetley, guest beer	
ROOMS: 4 en suite	

Food

Along with a range of curries, salads, cold and hot baguettes and burgers, the lunch menu offers gammon, egg and chips, steak pie, and in the evening, surf and turf and lamb cutlets. Separate restaurant menu.

Family facilities

Children are welcome inside the pub, and younger family members have their own menu.

Alternative refreshment stops

The Punchbowl in Askham, café and the Mardale Inn at Bampton, and the Crown and Mitre in Bampton Grange.

☛ Where to go from here

Rheged, at Redhills, near Penrith, is named after Cumbria's Celtic kingdom, and is a state-of-the-art attraction buried under a man-made hill, complete with a huge cinema screen and a mountaineering exhibition (www.rheged.com).

A sculpture trail from Rowrah

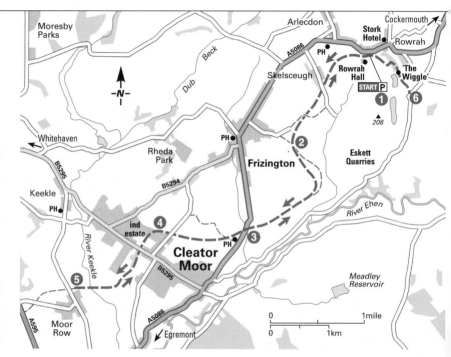

An easy linear ride along a sculpture trail, rich in industrial heritage.

Sculptures and wild flowers

The sculptures scattered along this route are a source of constant interest, with a personal favourite in the great crown-like arrangement of iron and timber on the elevated section. Get more information on all the sculptures from the Sustrans website, www.sustrans.org.uk: click on 'Interactive Mapping'.

Near the final turn (Point 6), you'll see a sign for High Leas nature reserve. It consists of five pristine wildflower meadows – now a very rare sight – and a fragment of an ancient agricultural system. They are home to several species of orchid, and the two lower fields also have lady's mantle and adder's-tongue. It's interesting to contrast these flower-rich fields with those on the other side of the track.

The cutting below Frizington is one of the most interesting sections of the route. The banks on the east side, which are relatively sunny, are covered in flowers through spring and summer. Notable are the fluffy purple-blue heads of scabious, much loved by butterflies such as the red admiral.

A bicycle propped against a National Cycle Network sign at Rowrah

Also present are vivid blue speedwell and wild strawberry. The opposite wall, which is much shadier and consequently damper, supports masses of ferns. A common species, with delicate dark green fronds, is maidenhair spleenwort, and the nearby station platform is overrun with it.

The cave in this cutting is not specially salubrious, but worth a quick look. The reddish colour and 'soapy' texture of the rock indicate the presence of haematite, the main ore mineral for the iron industry. This cave would have been a trial dig to see if the iron concentration improved.

the ride

1 Turn right out of the car park and back up the bumpy track, then keep straight on past the bridge and down a surfaced track on to the **railway line** proper. Follow

1h30 — **11.5 MILES** — **18.5 KM** — **LEVEL 1**23

MAP: OS Explorer OL 4 The English Lakes (NW) or OS Explorer 303 Whitehaven and Workington

START/FINISH: car park at Rowrah; grid ref: NY056185

TRAILS/TRACKS: almost entirely on good gritty tracks

LANDSCAPE: rolling farmland and woodland, views to fells

PUBLIC TOILETS: none on route

TOURIST INFORMATION: Whitehaven, tel 01946 852939

CYCLE HIRE: Ainfield Cycle Centre, Cleator, tel 01946 812427; Mark Taylor Cycles, Whitehaven, tel 01946 692252

THE PUB: Stork Hotel, Rowrah, near start of route

Getting to the start

Rowrah is 9 miles (14.5km) south of Cockermouth on the A5086. On a slight bend at the south end of the village (just before the sign for Arlecdon) is a track off to the left, signposted to Rowrah Hall and 'Cycleway car park'. Follow this over a bridge then turn left on a rough track. Take care here as this is part of the cycle route. In 150yds (137m) there is an open space on the left; park here.

Why do this cycle ride?

This ride is so packed with interest that its out-and-back nature is a positive advantage. It allows you two chances to enjoy the wayside flowers, two chances to admire the views in the middle section, and a second chance to see if you missed any sculptures the first time around.

Researched and written by: Jon Sparks

Rowrah **CUMBRIA**

this past the old station platforms below **Skelsceugh**, and about 1 mile (1.6km) further on reach a junction.

2 Bear right over a little **bridge** (the other branch doubles back under this and up to Frizington). A direction marker points you to Cleator Moor, Moor Row and Whitehaven. Continue along the trackbed, past more crumbling platforms, and then into a shady tree-lined cutting. There's exposed limestone rock in places and a small cave. Emerge onto a contrasting elevated section, with more expansive views, especially left towards the valley of **Ennerdale** and its surrounding fells. Go through another wooded section and cross an iron-railed bridge over the **A5086**.

3 Just after this a large **boulder** beside the track shows all the signs of having been shaped by ice – look for the striations (gouges) made by rocks embedded in the base of the glacier. A track then crosses the route: it takes some skill to negotiate the barriers here without putting a foot down. Continue along a stretch where the trees meet overhead, and keep ahead until the surfaced track runs out.

4 Bear half left (signed for Cleator Moor, Moor Row and Whitehaven), continue past an **industrial estate**, and under a road with finely decorated bridge arches. Keep straight on, signed to Moor Row and Whitehaven, following the main line of the track, guided by more signs for **Whitehaven**, until you reach another old station platform, with some interesting **sculptures**. Beyond this the surroundings become more urban, so it's a good turnaround point. (However, you can continue all the way into Whitehaven if you wish.)

5 On the return see if you missed any sculptures. Some are quite unassuming, like the seat built into one of the old platforms, or the squirrels and owls on top of wooden fence posts on the outskirts of Cleator Moor.

When you get back to the **car park** it's well worth continuing on the track, forking right past a barrier. Follow the track through a cutting with some exposed rock, then loop round left to avoid some old quarry workings (these are partly flooded – heed the warning signs). This takes you through '**The Wiggle**', a sculpture of curved stone walls by Robert Drake. Cross a small **bridge** and in the woods beyond, watch out for red squirrels. Pass another sculpture – two pieces of rock taken from the same block. Beyond this the path may be muddy in winter. A **National Cycle Network sign** tells you that it's 21 miles (33.8km) to Keswick and 120 miles (193km) to Sunderland, and the route rises to meet a lane. Go up the rise to see if you can work out the puzzle of the pedestrian gate alongside the small cattle grid for bikes – the instructions are all in symbols.

6 Turn around here to return to the **car park**.

A wayside sculpture with Crag Fell in the distance

Stork Hotel

about the pub

Stork Hotel

Rowrah Road, Rowrah
Frizington, Cumbria CA26 3XJ
Tel 01946 861213

DIRECTIONS: on the main road through the village

PARKING: 6

OPEN: daily, except Monday lunchtime

FOOD: Tuesday to Sunday

BREWERY/COMPANY: free house

REAL ALE: Jennings, Banks's, changing guest ales

ROOMS: 6 bedrooms

The Stork is only five minutes' walk from the cycleway car park (we say 'walk' advisedly, because the busy road is not comfortable for family cycling). It's not a place that gives itself airs, but it does offer comfortable surroundings, a warm welcome, locally brewed Jennings beer and a wide range of reasonably priced pub food in generous portions. Though you might need to have cycled a little further before you feel entitled to a Stork 'Big Grill', which includes Sirloin steak, lamb chop, bacon chop, Cumberland sausage, black pudding and all the trimmings. There's a limited amount of outside seating, which is close to the road but does have super views to the fells.

Food

If you don't fancy the mammoth mixed grill, try the steak, creamy mushroom chicken bake or Cumberland stack. Ploughman's lunches and salads are also served.

Family facilities

The Stork is ideal for families. There are high chairs available for younger children and a 'grubs up' menu for smaller appetites – bangers and mash, burgers, pasta bolognaise. Small portions of meals on the main menu are also available.

Alternative refreshment stops

There is a pub at Parkside (on the A5086, Point 3) close to the halfway point; also pubs just off the route at Frizington and Cleator Moor.

☛ Where to go from here

See 19 different breeds of sheep at the Lakeland Sheep and Wool Centre, Cockermouth, plus sheepdog demonstrations in summer (www.sheep-woolcentre.co.uk).

Rowrah CUMBRIA

Wild Ennerdale

A ride through the forest beyond Ennerdale Water.

Ennerdale

Pillar Rock, southeast of the lake end, stands proud of the mountainside in a way that few other crags do, and has a distinct summit of its own. This was first reached in 1826 by a local shepherd, John Atkinson. If conditions are good there may well be climbers on the Rock – binoculars will help you spot them. Today the easiest routes to the top are considered as hard scrambling rather than rock-climbing, but over the years climbers have added many routes on the various faces, some of them very challenging.

Some forty years ago the legendary fellwalker Alfred Wainwright wrote, 'Afforestation in Ennerdale has cloaked the lower slopes...in a dark and funereal shroud of foreign trees'. But things are changing. The Forestry Commission now plants a wider diversity of trees in many of its forests, and in the upper reaches of Ennerdale things have gone much further.

The Wild Ennerdale project is slowly restoring much more natural woodland. It's worth reflecting that the bare slopes of rough grass are not entirely 'natural' either, but the result of centuries of farming, most notably overgrazing by sheep.

the ride

1 Turn left from the **car park**, rolling down to the shores of **Ennerdale Water**. The track runs beside the lake for about 1 mile (1.6km), then continues through the forest above the river, here called **Char Dub**. Dub is a common dialect word for a pool, and the char is a species of fish. Continue past **Low Gillerthwaite Field Centre** and then the youth hostel at **High Gillerthwaite**.

2 Just past the youth hostel the track forks. Keep right (really straight ahead). The track goes up and down more than you might expect. Take care on fast downhill bends where the surface is loose. Above all don't grab at the brakes. At the next fork 1 mile (1.6km) further on, a sign to the right

2h00	12 MILES	19.3 KM	LEVEL 1 2 3

points to Pillar. Save the Pillar road for the return and keep straight on – in fact, this track straight ahead gives the best views of the **Pillar Rock**. The way climbs gradually to a more level stretch with open views across the valley to Pillar directly opposite. Pillar Rock is the centrepiece of a mass of crags strewn across the north face of the mountain. This is a worthy objective in itself and makes a reasonable turnaround point for those who feel they've gone far enough.

3 As Pillar falls behind, the valley head opens up. There's a space where you may find some vehicles and then the main track curves down right.

4 Straight ahead through a gate is a much rougher track leading 400yds (366m) to **Black Sail Hut Youth Hostel** – many people may prefer to walk for some or all of it. You can make yourself a cup of tea or coffee in the members' kitchen, but don't forget to leave a suitable donation. Return to the gate. The bridleway going up right climbs to Scarth Gap Pass and then descends to Buttermere. Ignore it, and go back through the gate and down left to the **River Liza**.

5 Splash through the concrete ford and swing round right. Now keep straight along the track, mostly downhill, ignoring branches up and left until it swings down to the **river**.

6 Cross the bridge and go up to the 'Pillar' signpost. Rejoin the main track of the outward route to return to the **car park**.

Top: Walkers beside Ennerdale Water
Left: Flowers on a rocky niche above Ennerdale Water

MAP: OS Explorer OL 4 The English Lakes (NW)

START/FINISH: Bowness Knott car park; grid ref: NY109153

TRAILS/TRACKS: good forest roads, occasionally bumpy

LANDSCAPE: lake, forest, wild valley ringed by high fells

PUBLIC TOILETS: none on route

TOURIST INFORMATION: Egremont, tel 01946 820693

CYCLE HIRE: Ainfield Cycle Centre, Cleator, tel 01946 812427; Mark Taylor Cycles, Whitehaven, tel 01946 692252

THE PUB: Shepherds Arms Hotel, Ennerdale Bridge, near the route

Rough track on the last short section (400yds/366m) to Black Sail Hut – mountain bike and some skill required, or walk. Suitability: children 10+. Younger children will enjoy a shorter version

Getting to the start
The car park is half way along the north shore of Ennerdale Water, at a dead-end. Access is via minor roads east from Ennerdale Bridge or south from Lamplugh.

Why do this cycle ride?
Although relatively gentle in itself, this route joins the world of the mountaineer, the fell-runner and the long-distance walker, entering the heart of the high fells. At the head of the valley, lonely Black Sail Hut Youth Hostel makes a perfect place to stop. You can make yourself a cup of tea there and even stay the night – but make sure that you book in advance (tel 0411 108450, not open all year).

Researched and written by: Jon Sparks

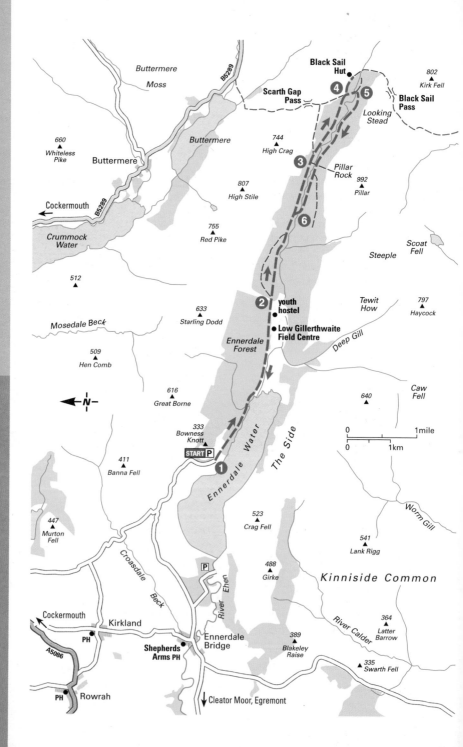

Buttermere
Moss

Black Sail Hut

802 ▲ Kirk Fell

Scarth Gap Pass

④ ⑤

Black Sail Pass

Looking Stead

660 ▲ Whiteless Pike

Buttermere

Buttermere

744 ▲ High Crag

③

Pillar Rock

992 ▲ Pillar

Cockermouth

807 ▲ High Stile

Crummock Water

755 ▲ Red Pike

⑥

Scoat Fell

Steeple

512 ▲

Tewit How

797 ▲ Haycock

Mosedale Beck

633 ▲ Starling Dodd

② ● youth hostel

● Low Gillerthwaite Field Centre

Deep Gill

509 ▲ Hen Comb

Ennerdale Forest

616 ▲ Great Borne

640 ▲

Caw Fell

←-N-→

333 ▲ Bowness Knott

START P

①

Ennerdale Water

The Side

0 ————— 1mile
0 ————— 1km

411 ▲ Banna Fell

523 ▲ Crag Fell

Worm Gill

447 ▲ Murton Fell

541 ▲ Lank Rigg

P

488 ▲ Girke

Kinniside Common

Croasdale Beck

River Ehen

364 ▲ Latter Barrow

River Calder

Cockermouth

Kirkland

PH

Ennerdale Bridge

389 ▲ Blakeley Raise

335 ▲ Swarth Fell

A5086

Shepherds Arms PH

↓ Cleator Moor, Egremont

PH Rowrah

46

Shepherds Arms Hotel

The Shepherds Arms Hotel sits at the heart of the village of Ennerdale Bridge, smack on the Coast-to-Coast route. This cream-washed country inn is welcoming and homely, its traditionally furnished bar (wood floors, bookcases, open log fires) dispense cracking real ales and hearty, home-cooked food to refuel the weariest of cyclists. In fact, walkers and cyclists are important here, evidenced by the maps posted in the bar, and the weather forecast chalked up daily on a blackboard. In addition, the en suite bedrooms are very comfortable, with period furnishings and pleasant views, and a restful night's sleep is guaranteed.

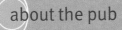

about the pub

Shepherds Arms Hotel
Ennerdale Bridge
Cumbria CA23 3AR
Tel 01946 861249
www.shepherdsarmshotel.co.uk

DIRECTIONS: in the centre of the village, 3.5 miles (5.7km) west of the start of the ride

PARKING: 6 (good street parking)

OPEN: daily, all day

FOOD: daily, lunchtime and evenings

BREWERY/COMPANY: free house

REAL ALE: Timothy Taylor Landlord, Coniston Bluebird, Jennings Bitter, guest beers

ROOMS: 8 bedrooms (6 en suite)

Food

From the bar menu, tuck into spinach and Wensleydale tart, local lamb chops, steak and ale pie with a suet crust, served with hand-cut chips or opt for something lighter like a warming bowl of soup, freshly made sandwiches and decent salads.

Family facilities

Children are welcome in the bars and overnight, with plenty of games and toys to keep them amused. There's a delightful garden, although it does border a fast-flowing stream, so supervision is necessary.

Alternative refreshment stops

None on route, although those venturing to Black Sail Youth Hostel (Point 4) can make themselves tea and coffee in the member's kitchen (donations).

☞ Where to go from here

The ruined 12th-century Egremont Castle is well worth a visit for its impressive red sandstone gatehouse. At the Florence Mine Heritage Centre just off the A595 you can tour the pit and see reconstructions of 19th-century pit life in the visitor centre.

Ennerdale CUMBRIA

A circuit from Wast Water to Stanton Bridge

Left: Cyclists on the route above Wast Water
Page 51: Scafell and Great Gable

of generations since. But only with very sharp eyes, or binoculars, and even then only in favourable light, are you likely to discern the natural obelisk called Napes Needle. Its first ascent in 1886 is often regarded as the birth of rock-climbing. It features in a memorial window in the lovely little church at Wasdale Head.

the ride

A pleasant rural ride with a short option and a magnificent scenic finale.

Wast Water

Wast Water is England's deepest lake, reaching a maximum depth of almost 260ft (79m), which means that its bed is well below sea level. The steep slope of The Screes, which face you across the lake, is continued deep underwater. The Screes, below the two summits of Whin Rigg and Illgill Head, are composed of decaying crags and masses of loose rock and boulders. This is landscape that is still evolving. There is a path, which you may be able to make out, running along the base of The Screes just above the level of the lake. It is no surprise to find that it is extremely rough going in places.

Looking up to the head of the lake and at the centre of the view (and of the National Park logo) is the pyramidal peak of Great Gable, 2,949ft (899m) high. High on its slopes facing you are the Napes Crags, beloved of the earliest rock-climbers and

1 Head west along the road towards **Gosforth**, climbing slightly and passing close under the craggy slopes of **Buckbarrow**. Climb a little more and then descend to a junction.

2 For the shorter loop, go left here, signed for Nether Wasdale. Follow the narrow lane and descend to a junction. Keep left and descend quite steeply into **Nether Wasdale**, levelling out at the village green, with **The Screes Inn** on the left and the **Strands Hotel** on the right (Point 5). For the longer ride, continue straight ahead at Point 2 and go straight on at the next junction. The road is fairly level, with views over the valley of the **River Irt** to the left and wooded slopes on the right. A little over 1 mile (1.6km) from the last junction, look for a bridleway on the left, signed for Hall Bolton.

3 Turn left onto the bridleway. The initial descent from the road is as rough as it gets. Keep right where the track forks and go straight ahead between the buildings at **Rainors**. Wind down to an attractive bridge over the **River Bleng**. Beyond this there's a short grassy section, then join the surfaced drive to **Hall Bolton**. Turn right and follow the drive out to a road. Turn left. Note, this track is rarely very muddy, but after wet weather you risk a soaking on the grassy section beyond the bridge. To avoid this, continue along the road at Point 3 over a small climb and then down steeply to **Wellington Bridge** and the outskirts of **Gosforth**. Bear left on a farm lane (bridleway) through **Row Farm** and on to **Rowend Bridge**. Turn left to follow the road to Santon Bridge. This adds about 1 mile (1.6km) to the total distance. Follow the road easily to **Santon Bridge**, past the pub and over the bridge.

4 Turn left on a narrow road past a campsite and soon begin a steeper climb at **Greengate Wood**. The gradient eases and the views ahead start to include the craggy outline of **The Screes**. Descend gently to **Forest Bridge**, then keep left, over **Cinderdale Bridge**, into **Nether Wasdale**. Follow the level road into the village and its twin pubs.

5 Retrace to **Cinderdale Bridge**, then keep left on the lane, signed to Wasdale Head. There are glimpses of The Screes and then of the lake, but trees screen them as you pass the youth hostel at **Wasdale Hall** and it's only when you cross a cattle grid to open fellside that the full panorama hits you. Follow the road down and then up a short climb to near a **cross-wall shelter** on the right, which commands a great view.

6 Continue down to cross **Countess Beck** and then turn left. It's now little more than a 0.25 mile (400m) cycle ride back to the start of the route.

2h00 — **11.25 MILES** — **18.1 KM** — **LEVEL 1 2 3**

SHORTER ALTERNATIVE ROUTE

1h00 — **5 MILES** — **8 KM** — **LEVEL 1 2 3**

MAP: OS Explorer OL 6 The English Lakes (SW)

START/FINISH: by Wast Water, roadside parking at Greendale; grid ref: NY144057

TRAILS/TRACKS: lanes; longer route has a short section of grassy bridleway

LANDSCAPE: wooded farmland then open fellside with view of lake and high fells

PUBLIC TOILETS: Gosforth

TOURIST INFORMATION: Ravenglass, tel 01229 717278; Sellafield, tel 019467 76510

CYCLE HIRE: Ainfield Cycle Centre, Cleator, tel 01946 812427; Mark Taylor Cycles, Whitehaven, tel 01946 692252

THE PUB: The Screes Inn, Nether Wasdale, see Point **5** on route

🚴 Some ascents and descents on both routes. Shorter loop, suitability: children 8+. Longer loop, suitability: children 11+

Getting to the start

Head east from Gosforth, pass a car park, then keep left on the Wasdale road. Follow this for 3 miles (4.8km) then keep left, signed to Wasdale Head for 2.5 miles (4km). Park in a grassy area on the left just past Greendale.

Why do this cycle ride?

The magnificent view of high fells around the head of Wast Water inspired the Lake District National Park logo, and would win many votes for the finest view in England. The ride saves this until near the end, first exploring the gentler scenery around Nether Wasdale.

Researched and written by: Jon Sparks

Wast Water

CUMBRIA

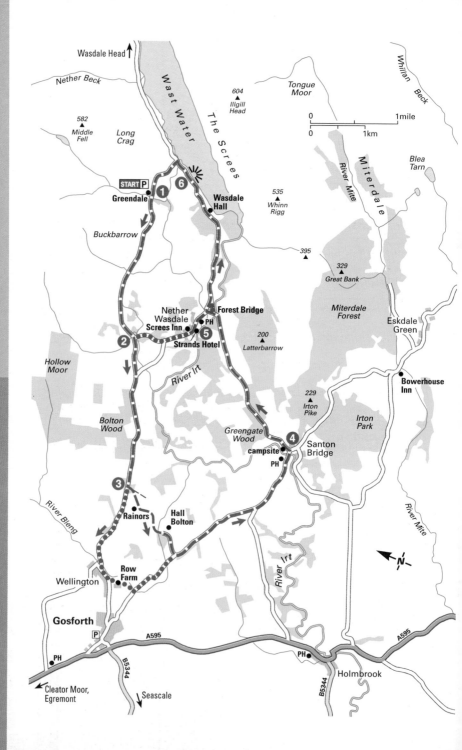

West Water CUMBRIA

Wasdale Head

Nether Beck

West Water

The Screes

604 ▲ Illgill Head

Tongue Moor

Whillan Beck

0 _____ 1mile
0 _____ 1km

582 ▲ Middle Fell

Long Crag

Blea Tarn

START P ❶ ❻

Greendale

Wasdale Hall

535 ▲ Whinn Rigg

River Mite

Miterdale

Buckbarrow

395 ▲

329 ▲ Great Bank

Miterdale Forest

Eskdale Green

Nether Wasdale Screes Inn Forest Bridge

PH

❷ ❺ Strands Hotel

200 ▲ Latterbarrow

Hollow Moor

River Irt

Bowerhouse Inn

Bolton Wood

229 ▲ Irton Pike

Irton Park

River Bleng

Greengate Wood

❹ Santon Bridge

campsite

PH

❸

Rainors

Hall Bolton

River Irt

River Mite

Row Farm

Wellington

Gosforth

P

A595

N

B5344

PH

PH

Holmbrook

Cleator Moor, Egremont

Seascale

B5344

A595

The Screes Inn

about the pub

The Screes Inn
Nether Wasdale, Seascale
Cumbria CA20 1ET
Tel 019467 26262
www.thescreesinnwasdale.com

DIRECTIONS: on the main road through the village, west of the church

PARKING: 20

OPEN: daily, all day

FOOD: daily

BREWERY/COMPANY: free house

REAL ALE: Black Sheep Bitter, Coniston Bluebird, Yates's Bitter, guest beer

ROOMS: 5 en suite

Two pubs face each other across the lane through Nether Wasdale, but both are owned by the same people. To pick one over the other may be invidious, but the 300-year-old Screes Inn does have one or two advantages: it's easy to park your bikes in sight of the outdoor tables, and it's open all day. Outside seating is separated from the road by an expanse of grass – a sort of village green – with a sunny aspect and glimpses of the fells lining Wasdale. Inside, it's a typically rambling Lakeland pub. The bars are partly slate-floored, and there's usually a log fire crackling in the grate – the perfect spot to savour a pint of Yates's bitter. Bike storage for overnight visitors.

Food
Specials from the blackboard might include smoked haddock, leek and potato pasties or Mexican wraps. Alternatively, try Woodall's Cumberland sausage with apple sauce, lasagne or steak and kidney pie from the local bakery. Vegetarians are well looked after as The Screes has a vegetarian chef.

Family facilities
Families will find a separate family room for the children to relax in. Small portions of main menu dishes are available (young children have their own menu), and there is plenty of good outdoor seating.

Alternative refreshment stops
The Strands Hotel in Nether Wasdale and, on the longer ride, the Bridge Inn at Stanton Bridge.

☞ Where to go from here
St Olaf's Church at Wasdale Head is one of England's smallest, and in its cemetery are the graves of several rock-climbers. This village became known as the birthplace of rock-climbing in Britain in the 1880s.

Woods and water by Windermere

Along the peaceful western shore of England's largest lake.

Windermere

Windermere was once the only lake in the Lake District without a speed limit, but a 10mph (16.1km) limit for powered craft on the lake came into force in 2005, helping to make this ride much more peaceful than previously. Other water traffic includes yachts of all sizes, windsurfers, canoes, rowing boats and the traditional launches and steamers which ply up and down throughout the year.

An attractive feature, the privately owned Belle Isle is said to have been used since Roman times. Today it is supplied by a little boat, which serves the 38 acre (15ha) estate. Belle Isle's circular house, recently rebuilt after extensive fire damage, was originally built by a Mr English in 1774. Apparently William Wordsworth accredited Mr English with the honour of being the first man to settle in the Lake District for the sake of the scenery.

The woodland here is typical of the Lake District. Before clearances for agriculture, notably sheep-grazing, there were many more similar woods. The predominant species is the sessile oak, which in times past provided timber for local industry and bark for tanning. It is a close relative of the 'English' oak of more southern counties, and it is not easy to tell them apart, but on closer inspection you will see that the acorns have no stalks to speak of. These woods are also rich in mosses and ferns, but often the most striking plant to be found is the foxglove, which fills the clearings.

the ride

1 Leave the **car park** and turn left on a surfaced lane. There are views along here of moored yachts, **Belle Isle** and the lake, with a backdrop of high fells. The shapely peak is **Ill Bell**. Follow the lane past lay-bys to reach a gate and cattle grid.

2 The road beyond is marked 'Unsuitable for Motor Vehicles'. Keep left past the entrance to **Strawberry Gardens**. Beyond this the track becomes considerably rougher, and soon begins to climb quite steeply. It's worth persevering!

3 Once over the crest and just as you begin to descend, look out on the left

1h00 — **5.75 MILES** — **9.2 KM** — **LEVEL 123**

MAP: OS Explorer OL 7 The English Lakes (SE)

START/FINISH: car park near Windermere Ferry; grid ref: SD387958

TRAILS/TRACKS: mostly easy tracks, some stony sections

LANDSCAPE: rich woodland and lakeshore

PUBLIC TOILETS: none on route

TOURIST INFORMATION: Bowness-on-Windermere, tel 015394 42895

CYCLE HIRE: Wheelbase, Staveley, tel 01539 821443; Bike Treks, Ambleside, tel 01539 431245; Ghyllside Cycles, Ambleside, tel 01539 433592; Grizedale Mountain Bikes, Grizedale Forest, tel 01229 860369

THE PUB: Sawrey Hotel, Far Sawrey, near start of route

🛈 Mostly easy but one rough steep climb and descent. Suitability: children 8+. Mountain bike recommended, or walk some sections. Shorter ride from Red Nab, all ages

Getting to the start

Road access to Windermere's mid-western shore is via Far Sawrey or on minor roads from the south. Follow the B5285 towards the ferry terminal, turning left up a lane before the terminal itself, to reach a National Trust car park. Alternatively, bring your bikes over by ferry from Bowness-on-Windermere.

Why do this cycle ride?

This is a perfect ride for taking a picnic. The full ride is surprisingly challenging, with a steep, rocky climb and descent halfway, though elsewhere the going is easy. For a shorter ride, go from the car park at Red Nab, then follow the bridleway to High Wray Bay.

for a **wildlife viewing platform**. There are squirrel feeders scattered in the trees, and you may spot roe deer. Take great care on the descent – there are loose stones and several rocky steps, and it may be safer to walk down. The track levels out for a short distance, then continues its descent, finally levelling out just above the lakeshore. The going is easier now, generally level. Pass several small **shingle beaches**. Keep left (almost straight ahead) at a fork and then, where a bridleway climbs off to the left, keep right (signed to **Red Nab** and **Wray**) along a smoother gravel track. At a gate, emerge onto a tarmac track but almost immediately fork right, signposted 'Bridleway Wray Castle'. Continue into the **Red Nab car park**.

Above: Windermere seen from Orrest Head

Researched and written by: Jon Sparks

4 Go round a low barrier on to the bridleway. This is level, easy riding all the way along to a gate by a boathouse, beyond which you emerge to the curve of **High Wray Bay**. The bridleway now veers away from the lake. The bay is a popular picnic spot, with people arriving both by land and by water. Walk the bikes round to the grassy slope above the further shore.

5 Retrace your route to Point 2.

6 A bridleway rises off to the right here. It offers the option of a direct route to the pub at **Far Sawrey**, but the climb is longer, steeper and rougher than what you have encountered so far – so unless you found that all too easy, it's best to ignore it and simply return to the **car park**. The road route to the pub requires riding for 1 mile (1.6km) on the **B5285**, which can be busy at times, and also involves a steep climb midway.

Tree-covered hills sloping down to Windermere from Gummers How

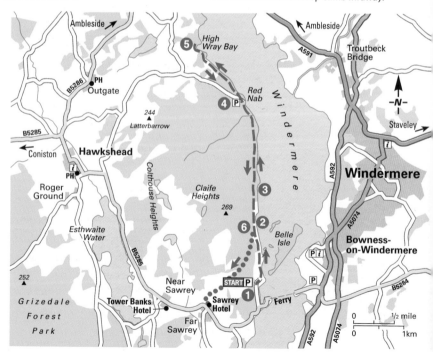

Sawrey Hotel

The Sawrey Hotel unites three original buildings into a remarkably harmonious whole. The oldest part, on the left of the current hotel entrance, dates back to around 1700. To the left again is the former stable block, altered in 1971 to form the Claife Crier Bar. This gets its name from a ghostly local legend, illustrated on the sign above the door. Some of the original stalls have been retained, making attractive and secluded seating areas, and the old beams are believed to have come from ships wrecked on the Cumbrian coast. Original horse-collars and other memorabilia decorate the walls. Outside is a pleasant garden, which keeps the sun until late in the evening and has stunning views to Coniston Old Man and Swirl How.

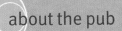

about the pub

Sawrey Hotel
Far Sawrey, Ambleside
Cumbria LA22 0LQ
Tel 015394 43425

DIRECTIONS: on the B5285

PARKING: 30

OPEN: daily, all day

FOOD: daily

BREWERY/COMPANY: free house

REAL ALE: Black Sheep Bitter, Theakston's Best, Hawkshead Bitter, Jennings Cumberland Ale, guest beer

ROOMS: 19 en suite

Food
Bar lunches include smoked salmon sandwiches, a Hiker's lunch (cheddar cheese), local venison sausage with tomato and apple chutney, and beef casserole. Set dinner menu only.

Family facilities
Children are welcome in the bar until 9pm, and allowed in the lounge at all times. At lunch, younger children have their own menu, and older children can chose smaller portions of some adult dishes. Safe garden.

Alternative refreshment stops
None along the route. The New Inn at Far Sawrey and Tower Banks Arms in Sawrey.

☛ Where to go from here
Hill Top is the 17th-century farmhouse at Near Sawrey where Beatrix Potter wrote and illustrated her tales of Peter Rabbit and his friends (tel 015394 36269; www.nationaltrust.org.uk).

Grizedale Forest Park and Satterthwaite

Cycle along a great circuit of the forest park.

Grizedale Forest
The speed and near-silence of a bike sometimes gives you some great wildlife encounters. We were privileged to see a family of foxes playing in the first few miles of this route. This may be exceptional, but deer – both red and roe – are widespread in the forest, and the sight of a buzzard overhead is almost guaranteed. (Buzzards are occasionally mistaken for eagles, but if you see a large bird of prey circling over this forest, it's a buzzard.) In spring the

courtship flights of these big birds of prey are beautiful to watch, and you may also occasionally see them being mobbed or harassed by other birds.

In the second half of the route there are great views west to the Coniston Fells. The principal peak at the southern end of the range is the Coniston Old Man (originally Allt Maen, meaning a high stone or cairn). To its left you glimpse the rock buttresses of Dow Crag, one of the great rock-climbers' crags of England. The sides of the Coniston Fells are heavily scarred, most obviously by slate quarries, but also by the copper mines which worked for around 500 years, reaching their peak in the 19th century.

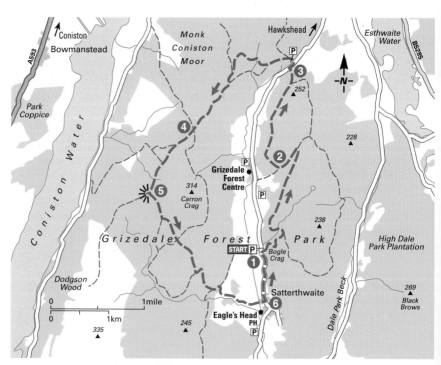

Cycling along a trail in Grizedale Forest

2h00 **9.5 MILES** **15.3 KM** **LEVEL 123**

MAP: OS Explorer OL 7 The English Lakes (SE)
START/FINISH: Bogle Crag car park, Grizedale Forest; grid ref: SD337933
TRAILS/TRACKS: forest tracks with mostly good surface, short sections of field track and lane
LANDSCAPE: forest, with views to the fells
PUBLIC TOILETS: Grizedale Forest Centre
TOURIST INFORMATION: Hawkshead, tel 015394 36525
CYCLE HIRE: Grizedale Mountain Bikes, Grizedale, tel 01229 860369
THE PUB: The Eagles Head, Satterthwaite, see Point **6** on route
🅵 Some moderately steep descents with loose surfaces. Suitability: children 12+. Mountain bike recommended. (Other waymarked routes in the forest are shorter and easier)

the ride

1 At the top of **Bogle Crag car park** go round the barrier and straight up the rocky track at a steady gradient. At a junction of tracks bear left, and enjoy a brief downhill respite and a fairly level section before some more steady climbing, sustained but never really steep. Where this eases off, turn left (**purple route marker**).

2 At the next fork keep right on the easy forest road, which sweeps round to the right (the left branch is a bridleway which makes a steep, rocky, experts-only descent direct to the Grizedale Forest visitor centre). After some undulations there's a longer downhill, then another substantial climb, quite steep to start. Just over the top, reach a junction of tracks. Go left and gently downhill to a **gate**. The most challenging part of the uphill section is now over.

3 Go round the gate on the left, with care as the ground is rocky. Come out to the road and turn right. After 200yds (183m) turn left at **Moor Top**. Go through the **car park** and immediately beyond the barrier

Getting to the start
Grizedale Forest lies to the east of Coniston Water, with the village of Grizedale at its heart. Bogle Crag car park is 0.75 mile (1.2km) south of the village on the only road through the valley, and 0.5 mile (800m) north of Satterthwaite.

Why do this cycle ride?
Grizedale Forest Park has many waymarked cycle routes on the forest roads, as well as a pre-existing network of bridleways, some of which offer much tougher riding (strictly for hardened mountain-bikers). The route makes for a fine day out, and gives a fair sample of what the forest has to offer.

Researched and written by: Jon Sparks

Grizedale CUMBRIA

57

fork left. Pass a small lake (**Juniper Tarn**) in the trees on the left and at the next fork go right. Curve round the head of a small valley and climb fairly gently, keeping straight on where another track joins from the right. At the next junction keep right. The next section is broadly level, past stands of **younger trees**. Pass an area of broadleaf planting (mostly birch) and get the first view of the **Coniston Fells** away to the right. Continue, to reach a double junction, almost a crossroads.

4 Bear left and then right to maintain the same general direction. Keep on along the **main track**, past several turnings descending to the right, until an obvious track forks off down to the right. There's a **bench** here, with a great view of the full length of the **Coniston Fells**. It's a perfect place to pause for a drink or snack, or just to enjoy the panorama.

5 Ignore the descending track and keep on along the level one. Soon there's a small rise and the track swings round to the left. A bridleway breaks off to the right here – another classic mountain bike route. Keep straight on and descend, passing another track that branches off to the right. At the next junction keep left (**green waymark**). This section is quite loose, so take care. Keep straight on at the next junction – a narrower track on the right makes it a crossroads. There's more fast descent through **mature forest** – the surface here is mostly good, but gets looser as you drop to a T-junction. Turn left and continue the descent, winding down through **broadleaf woods**. Keep left at the next junction, over a slight rise, then look out for a right turn (easy to miss) just before the track reaches fields on the right. Follow this slightly rougher track down to a gate and then through fields. It's bumpy in places as it descends to another gate, then continues across the level valley floor.

Sculpture of a man with an axe in the undergrowth at Grizedale Forest

The village of **Satterthwaite** is ahead. There's a short rise, with bedrock visible, before you meet the road.

6 Turn left here for a direct return to **Bogle Crag car park**, or turn right for 400yds (366m) to **The Eagles Head** pub.

The Eagles Head

about the pub

The Eagles Head
Satterthwaite, Ulverston
Cumbria LA12 8LN
Tel 01229 860237

DIRECTIONS: in the centre of the village, just south of the church
PARKING: 10
OPEN: closed Monday lunch (not Bank Hols)
FOOD: no food Monday evening
BREWERY/COMPANY: free house
REAL ALE: Eagles Head, Grizedale, Theakston's and guest ales

'Walkers and cyclists are always welcome, however muddy.' That comment sums up the unpretentious Eagles Head. And on some of the rougher routes in Grizedale, it is understood that mountain-bikers can get very muddy indeed. This fine pub says it is 'In the Heart of the Grizedale Forest', and that seems to be true in more senses than the purely geographical. The interior is warm and cosy in a style typical of many a Lakeland hostelry, complete with slate floor, log fires and simple furnishings. On a fine day there is intense competition for tables in the small but delightful garden, with its sheltering trees and flower-decked walls. Additional attractions include tip-top local ales.

Food

There are separate lunchtime and evening menus, with good quality sandwiches (home-roast ham and cheese), filled jacket potatoes and leek and mushroom crumble at lunchtime. Some main course dishes, like home-made steak, chicken or game pies, made with famously good shortcrust pastry, overlap on both menus, but the evening selection ranges more widely, with a good choice of curry dishes and some vegetarian options.

Family facilities

Families are welcome. Children's menu.

Alternative refreshment stops

Café at the Grizedale Forest visitor centre; pubs and cafés in nearby Hawkshead.

☞ Where to go from here

Admire an annually changing exhibition of Beatrix Potter's paintings used to illustrate her children's books, often incorporating local scenes, at the Beatrix Potter Gallery, Hawkshead (tel 015394 36355).

Grizedale CUMBRIA

Bouth and Oxen Park

An action-packed short ride, which has an exciting off-road option.

A wooded landscape

Magnificent woodland, dominated by sessile oak, is a major feature of this ride. Cyclists on the longer route who take the climb to Ickenthwaite will have plenty of time to appreciate this. In earlier times these woods were an industrial resource, providing raw materials for the bobbin industry and for charcoal-making to feed the many small iron makers in the area. Near the start of the ride, Moss Wood and the adjoining Height Springs Wood are now maintained by the

Woodland Trust. The track into Moss Wood is a bridleway so you could easily ride in a short way to get a closer look. You will see areas where the trees have been coppiced. This seemingly drastic operation involves cutting the tree back almost to ground level, but does not kill the plant. Instead it puts out many small shoots which in a few years provide thin timber ideal for both bobbin-making and charcoal-burning.

Just beyond the Manor House Inn in Oxen Park, you pass a grey barn-like building beside the road. Note the carved sign on the wall, which dates it to 1697, and portrays a selection of blacksmith's implements. Incidentally, a blacksmith is a general ironworker, who would largely have been involved in producing tools – one whose main job is shoeing horses is strictly called a farrier.

the ride

1 Follow the lane north, away from Bouth. Keep left at the first junction, signed to Oxen Park. The lane twists up through **woodland**, with a couple of quite sharp sections of climbing, passing the entrance to **Moss Wood**, before levelling out. At the next junction there is a triangle of grass.

The Vale of Colton, crossed by a narrow road

Below left: Cyclist on a track between dry-stone walls

2 For the shorter ride go left here, signed to Oxen Park. The road twists and descends, crosses a little valley, then begins a steep twisting climb. As climbs go, this is not too long. Over the top, freewheel a short way to a T-junction on the outskirts of Oxen Park. Turn left to rejoin the longer loop shortly after Point 5.

For the longer route, keep right at Point 2, signposted 'Rusland: Gated Road'. Follow this lane until it drops to a T-junction. There's no need, but those with mountain-biking blood in their veins may not be able to resist splashing through the ford under the trees just before the junction. Turn right on the wider road, signed to **Grizedale**, and follow it for 0.75 mile (1.2km). Shortly after passing the elegant **Whitestock Hall**, look for a sharp left turn, signed to Ickenthwaite.

3 This leads immediately into a very steep climb, so engage low gear in advance. The gradient eventually eases and then the woods give way to fields.

2h00 — **7.75 MILES** — **12.5 KM** — **LEVEL 123**

SHORTER ALTERNATIVE ROUTE

1h00 — **4.5 MILES** — **7.2 KM** — **LEVEL 123**

MAP: OS Explorer OL 7 The English Lakes (SE)

START/FINISH: lane north of Bouth; grid ref: SD328859

TRAILS/TRACKS: quiet lanes; rough tracks on longer ride, short challenging descents

LANDSCAPE: mix of woods and pasture, many small hills, views to higher fells

PUBLIC TOILETS: none on route

TOURIST INFORMATION: Ulverston, tel 01229 587120

CYCLE HIRE: South Lakeland Mountain Bike Sales & Hire, Lowick Bridge, Ulverston, tel 01229 885210; Wheelbase, Staveley, tel 01539 821443

THE PUB: White Hart Inn, Bouth, see Point **1** on route

🛑 Steep gradients on both loops. Shorter loop, suitability: children 7+. On longer loop, off-road descents require experience and skill, or walk short sections, suitability: children 12+. Mountain bike recommended

Getting to the start

Bouth is 1.25 miles (2km) north of the A590. Park in a grassy lay-by on the northern edge of the village, beyond the pub, or further along the lane on the first part of the ride.

Why do this cycle ride?

This short ride packs in a lot, in an area that's pure Lake District yet never inundated with visitors. For every climb there's a pleasant descent, and a new view to enjoy.

Researched and written by: Jon Sparks

Bouth CUMBRIA

61

4 Just after **Low Ickenthwaite** turn left on to a bridleway signed to Oxen Park. The track is initially stony with a good ribbon of grass down the middle. After a second gate it becomes stonier but is still straightforward. Stay close to the wall on the left, ignoring a couple of branch tracks. The track then climbs a bit on to an open, bracken-covered area. The best riding is generally in the centre of the track as the sides are quite rough. Go through another gate, and a little more climbing leads to the crest. Keep straight ahead at another fork and the track levels off. A short steep section at the start of the descent calls for some skill. If in doubt, walk down this. Then descend more steeply to another gate. The twisting descent beyond this is steep and loose and requires great care. Again, walk down rather than risk a nasty fall. Just beyond its foot is another gate.

5 Emerge on to a road and turn right into **Oxen Park**. As you enter the village, the shorter ride joins in from the left. Keep straight ahead through the village. The road begins a sweeping descent into the soft green **Vale of Colton**.

6 Just after the **Old Vicarage** turn left, signposted 'Colton Church and Bouth', up a short steep climb. At the crest another sign to Colton Church and Bouth points left, up a further climb. But this is an off-road route, so continue straight on. Descend to pass **Greenhead Farm**, and the road is fairly level along the valley side. Keep left through two junctions. The road curves and makes a steep final drop to a T-junction (take care). Go left for an almost level run along a broader road back through **Bouth**.

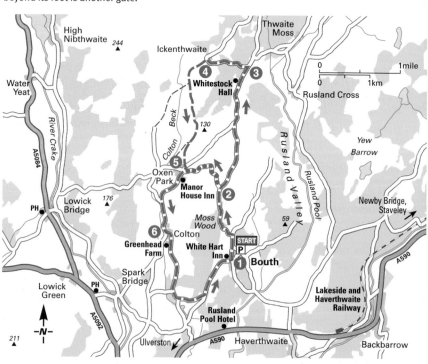

White Hart Inn

about the pub

White Hart Inn
Bouth, Ulverston
Cumbria LA12 8JB
Tel 01229 861229
www.edirectory.co.uk/whitehartinn

DIRECTIONS: in the middle of the village
PARKING: 30
OPEN: closed Monday and Tuesday
lunchtime; rest of week open all day
July–September
FOOD: daily
BREWERY/COMPANY: free house
REAL ALE: Jennings Cumberland Ale, Black
Sheep Bitter, Tetley, 3 guest beers
ROOMS: 4 en suite

A 16th-century former coaching inn, the
White Hart is in a quiet village among
woods, fields and fells. Sloping beamed
ceilings and floors in the main bar show
the building's age, while two log fires
help create a cosy and welcoming
atmosphere. Walls and ceilings are
festooned with bric-a-brac and old
photos – look out for the farm tools,
stuffed animals and long-stemmed clay
pipes. The landlord has a genuine
passion for real ale, with six great ales,
including brews from Cumbrian microbreweries, to draw the customers in.
He refuses to allow vinegar in the bar
as it 'affects the quality of the beer'.
A pub that has its priorities right!
Upstairs there's a more open feel to
the restaurant, with a large window
giving it a fine outlook, shared with the
rear terrace. The terrace has heaters for
those chillier days, and a pleasant view
of pastures and the wooded flanks of
Colton Fell.

Food
The menu offers fresh food cooked to order
using beef, pork and lamb from Abbots
Reading Farm, a few miles away. Typically,
this might include steak and stout pie,

lamb and apricot pie, and pork medallions
in port and mushroom sauce. Expect also
soups, salads and sandwiches.

Family facilities
Children are welcome in the eating areas
and games room, and there's a limited
children's menu. Play area on the village
green opposite.

Alternative refreshment stops
The Manor House pub in Oxen Park
(Point 5).

☞ Where to go from here
Lakeside is the steamer stop at the
southern end of Lake Windermere and the
starting point for the Lakeside and
Haverthwaite Railway (www.windermere
-lakecruises.co.uk). A short steam trip runs
to Haverthwaite and there's a small
collection of steam and diesel locomotives.
Next door the fascinating Aquarium of the
Lakes is well worth a visit
(www.aquariumofthelakes.co.uk).

Around the Winster Valley from Bowland Bridge

A loop through a delightful secluded valley, with minimal traffic.

The Winster Valley
The valley floor and the hills to the west are of slate, the ridges to the east of limestone. The strata in both cases generally dip down towards the east, and the younger limestone actually lies on top of the older slate.
The slate is part of what geologists call the Windermere Group of rocks and is roughly 400 million years old. The limestone – carboniferous limestone, to be precise – is 300–350 million years old, and quite young by geological standards (the most ancient rocks in Britain are nearly ten times as old).

The woods on the western slopes of the valley are dominated by oak, while on the limestone ash trees are more common, with many gnarled yew trees on steeper slopes and where the soil is thin. You can see some fine examples where the lane climbs the steep flank of Yewbarrow. Yews are tough, slow-growing, long-lived trees and able to survive where there seems to be hardly any soil. It is also worth knowing that yews are the best trees to shelter under when it rains, as their down-sloping leaves shed the water to the outside.

the ride

1 Follow the road, with the pub on your left, and cross the **bridge** that gives Bowland Bridge its name. Soon the road begins to climb quite steeply. Fortunately, you don't have to go too far up before you turn off to the left, signposted to Cartmel Fell and High Newton. There's a brief stretch of more level riding, then another short steep climb before you swoop down past the turning for **Cartmel Fell Church**. Continue straight on to meet a wider road at an angled junction.

2 Go straight across the junction on to a surfaced track over a cattle grid, signed to Ashes and Low Thorphinsty.

A cyclist negotiating a path lined with bushes and plants near Ashes in the Winster Valley

Go through **Ashes farmyard**. After another 100yds (91m) the way ahead is blocked by a gate. Turn left immediately before this, go through another gate and down a grassy track. After a second gate the grass gets longer, but it's only a short way further to a lane. While it's rarely muddy, the long grass will give you a good wetting after rain.

3 Turn right along the lane and follow it easily down the valley for 2 miles (3.2km) to a **crossroads** with an old-fashioned black-and-white **signpost**.

4 Turn left, signed to Witherslack. Climb slightly over the **Holme**, a slatey hump rising from the valley floor, then dip down again to **Bleacrag Bridge**. Bear left at the junction, at a triangle of grass, cycling on to a narrow lane which has remnants of grass down the middle. This lane gradually draws closer to the rocky limestone flanks of Yewbarrow, climbing into a dark tunnel of yew trees. There are lots of exposed roots in the thin soil, and the first close glimpses of the limestone. Another lane joins this one from the right.

The view south west across Winster Valley

1h30 — **9.5 MILES** — **15.3 KM** — **LEVEL 123**

MAP: OS Explorer OL 7 The English Lakes (SE)
START/FINISH: Bowland Bridge; grid ref: SD417896
TRAILS/TRACKS: quiet lanes, with a short optional section on grassy bridleway
LANDSCAPE: lush valley overlooked by limestone escarpment
PUBLIC TOILETS: none on route
TOURIST INFORMATION: Bowness-on-Windermere, tel 015394 42895
CYCLE HIRE: South Lakeland Mountain Bike Sales & Hire, Lowick Bridge, Ulverston, tel 01229 885210; Wheelbase, Staveley, tel 01539 821443
THE PUB: Hare & Hounds Country Inn, Bowland Bridge, see Point **1** on route
❶ Undulating ride with a few steep hills. Suitability: children 8+

Getting to the start
Bowland Bridge is a tiny village 1.75 miles (2.8km) south west of Crosthwaite, on a minor road between the A5074 and the A592. Park in the small lay-by opposite the Hare & Hounds Country Inn, or in others scattered along the first part of the route.

Why do this cycle ride?
Although close to main roads and to tourist honeypots like Bowness, the Winster Valley is remarkably quiet. It's a great place for a relaxing ride, with few worries about traffic and a better than average chance of sunshine – for the Lake District. Limestone crags overlook the lush valley floor with its outcrops of slate, a geological boundary that marks a contrast between the earlier and later stages of the ride.

Researched and written by: Jon Sparks

Winster Valley CUMBRIA

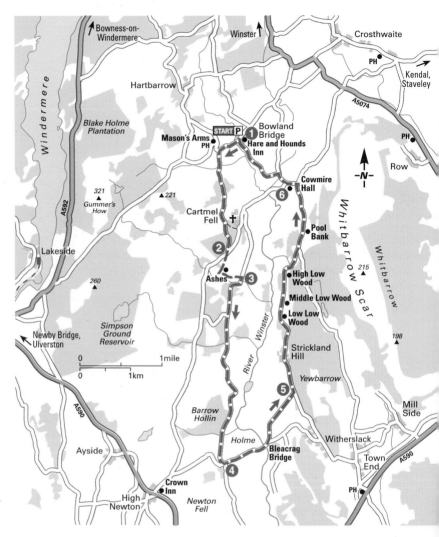

5 Continue along the lane past **Strickland Hill** and **Askew Green** until the way kinks through the farmyard of **Low Low Wood,** with a fine barn. Go through a gate ahead on to a rougher section of lane, past **Middle Low Wood** and **High Low Wood**. Climb to a T-junction and turn left. As you come over the crest and twist down past the beautiful **Pool Bank farm**, there's the best view yet of the steep flanks of the **Whitbarrow ridge** spreading out before you. At another grass triangle turn left, signed to Bowland Bridge.

6 Keep right past **Cowmire Hall,** swing round and drop down to another junction. Keep left here and go along the valley bottom near the river to reach the junction at **Bowland Bridge**. The **Hare & Hounds** is just to the right.

Hare & Hounds Country Inn

In the beautiful Winster Valley, with stunning views over Cartmel Fell, this 17th-century coaching inn is just 10 minutes' drive from the southern tip of Windermere. It's a truly rural, attractive building that successfully blends ancient and modern, with its rough stone walls, farming memorabilia and simple wooden furniture. Crackling log fires warm you in winter. On fine days head outside with your drinks and sit and survey the terrain covered by the ride. It's easy to overlook the orchard garden to the side of the pub, south-facing and enjoying views down the valley dominated by the crag-fringed ridge of Whitbarrow Scar. What better place to savour a pint from the ever-changing selection of real ales?

about the pub

Hare & Hounds Country Inn
Bowland Bridge, Grange-over-Sands
Cumbria LA11 6NN
Tel 015395 68333

DIRECTIONS: on the main road through the village

PARKING: 50

OPEN: closed Tuesday, open all day Saturday and Sunday

FOOD: daily

BREWERY/COMPANY: free house

REAL ALE: 4 changing guest beers

ROOMS: 1 en suite

Food

Satisfying bar meals include filled baps (Brie, bacon and cranberry), speciality Thai mussels with lemon grass, lime, chilli and fresh coriander, ploughman's lunches, fish pie and warm salads. Look to the seasonal menu for roast duck, shank of lamb, poached salmon and chargrilled steaks.

Family facilities

Children are welcome, and on summer days they can play on the swings in the garden.

Alternative refreshment stops

The Mason's Arms (great beer and super views) at top of Strawberry Bank near the start of the ride.

☞ Where to go from here

South east of Crossthwaite, Levens Hall is a fascinating Elizabethan house, noted for its plasterwork, panelling and topiary garden (tel 015395 60321).

Winster Valley

CUMBRIA

A circuit around Cartmel

Explore a handsome
valley between the fells
and the sea.

Cartmel

There have been buildings on the site
of Cartmel Priory for more than 800 years,
though only the church and the gatehouse
remain standing today. One of the most
striking features of the notably beautiful
church is the number of memorials to
travellers who lost their lives crossing
Morecambe Bay. In the days before
railways and modern roads, the sands
of the bay were in regular use by travellers
of all kinds, and an official Queen's Guide
was charged with ensuring their safety.

Those who dispensed with his services
risked blundering into quicksand or being
caught by the fast-advancing tides –
hazards which are still very real. The office
of Queen's Guide survives to this day, and
visitors are still guided safely across these
treacherous sands every year.

Horse racing at Cartmel also has
a long tradition behind it, and the race
meetings around the late May and August
bank holidays draw horses, jockeys and
punters from far and wide for an exciting
day out. However, busy roads on race
days mean these times are best avoided
by cyclists.

*The church at Cartmel Priory with its square
tower set diagonally*

the ride

1h00 **8 MILES** **12.9 KM** **LEVEL 1 2 3**

1 From the **racecourse** ride back into **Cartmel village square** and turn sharp left (round the village shop). This quickly takes you out of the village again and alongside the racecourse. Keep left at a junction, following signs for Haverthwaite and Ulverston, and begin a steady climb (never really steep). The road forks again at **Beck Side**.

2 Keep on to the right, still climbing steadily. The limestone arch on the right just above the fork is the remains of a **lime kiln**. There's a brief dip at **High Gateside**, another short rise, then turn right and begin an excellent swooping descent, with no tricky bends.

3 A turn on the right at a triangle of grass offers the option of a short return back to Cartmel. Otherwise, keep straight on here, and at a second junction, cross the tiny river of **Ayside Pool** (pool as the word for a river occurs several places hereabouts), then up slightly to reach a T-junction. Turn left on a broader road and continue for about 0.5 mile (800m), passing **Field Broughton church**, whose spire dominates the upper part of the valley just as Cartmel Priory does the lower.

4 At the next junction fork right, signed to **Barber Green**, and keep left where the road splits again. At a tiny crossroads under a spreading beech tree turn right, following signs for Barber Green. Ascend gently as

MAP: OS Explorer OL 7 The English Lakes (SE)

START/FINISH: Cartmel racecourse; grid ref: SD375791

TRAILS/TRACKS: country lanes, some wider roads. Avoid doing this ride when race meetings are on

LANDSCAPE: wide valley flanked by ridges, with views to the higher fells and to Morecambe Bay

PUBLIC TOILETS: Cartmel

TOURIST INFORMATION: Ulverston, tel: 01229 587120

CYCLE HIRE: South Lakeland Mountain Bike Sales and Hire, Lowick Bridge, Ulverston, tel: 01229 885210

THE PUB: Cavendish Arms, Cartmel, see Point **6** on route

! Railway path section is suitable for all ages. If continuing into Threlkeld, suitability: children 6+; if returning via stone circle there's a short section (walk on pavement) alongside busy A road, and crossing another. Suitability: children 10+

Getting to the start

Cartmel is 2 miles (3.2km) west of Grange-over-Sands. The racecourse is west of the village square, and there's an honesty-box at the car park there.

Why do this cycle ride?

The Vale of Cartmel is a classic English landscape, its skylines punctuated by nothing more obtrusive than a church tower. Add views of the high Lakeland fells and the shining expanse of Morecambe Bay, and there are few better rides for scenic variety.

Researched and written by: Jon Sparks

the road climbs more seriously again. Keep straight on at the crossroads just beyond the village. The next bit is steeper, but as you near the top there's a great view to the right down the valley, with the **tower** of the priory standing out and the sweep of Morecambe Bay beyond. Finally, the climb levels off. Just beyond this, reach a T-junction on the outskirts of **High Newton**.

5 Turn right and shortly keep right at a fork by the aptly named **Valley View**. Descend (another fine run) past **Head House**. Keep straight on at the crossroads of **Four Lane Ends**. After 0.5 mile (800m) reach an angled junction with a wider road. Keep left (almost straight ahead) for an easy run back to **Cartmel**.

6 About 200yds (183m) past the 30mph sign on the edge of Cartmel, turn right at an 'Unsuitable for heavy goods vehicles'

sign. Follow the narrowing lane between cottages and past the back of the **Priory**, then loop round and past the **Cavendish Arms**. Go under the gatehouse arch into the village square. Take the lane left of the village shop back to the **racecourse**.

Bust of Sir William Lowther, Cartmel Priory

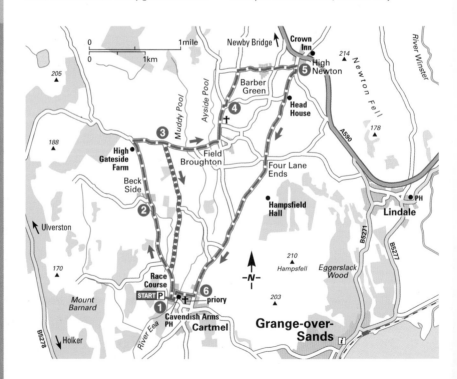

Cavendish Arms

Cartmel's oldest hostelry dates from the 15th century and stands tucked away from the village square. It is built within the old village walls and was once a thriving coaching stop, with stables where the bar is now. Note the mounting block dated 1837 outside the main door. The civilised main bar has low oak beams, a comfortable mixture of furnishings, Jennings ale on tap, a good selection of wines by glass or bottle, and welcoming log fires burn on cooler days. There is a separate non-smoking restaurant, and ten well appointed bedrooms.

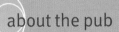

about the pub

Cavendish Arms
Cavendish Street, Cartmel
Grange-over-Sands,
Cumbria LA11 6QA
Tel 015395 36240
www.thecavendisharms.co.uk

DIRECTIONS: off the main square	
PARKING: 15	
OPEN: daily, all day	
FOOD: daily	
BREWERY/COMPANY: free house	
REAL ALE: Jennings Bitter, Wells Bombardier, guest beer	
ROOMS: 10 en suite	

Food
Bar food ranges from soup and sandwiches to lamb Henry, Cumberland sausages in a rich onion gravy and herb-crusted cod. The dessert menu includes Cartmel's speciality, sticky toffee pudding. Typical restaurant dishes might be fillet steak, sea bass and ostrich fillet.

Family facilities
Children are genuinely welcome. A children's menu is available, and the rear garden has small play area and a viewpoint from which to feed the ducks.

Alternative refreshment stops
Try the King's Arms, Royal Oak, Market Cross Cottage Tea Rooms or the Pig and Whistle Bistro in Cartmel. Close to the midpoint is the Crown Inn at High Newton.

☛ Where to go from here
There's plenty to see at Holker Hall, west of Cartmel at Cark, including magnificent gardens and the Lakeland Motor Museum (tel: 015395 58328; www.holker-hall.co.uk).

Glasson Dock to Lancaster

Follow the River Lune to explore Lancaster, and share the delights of its canal towpath on the way back.

Lancaster

LANCASHIRE

Wildlife along the way

Aldcliffe Marsh is a Site of Special Scientific Interest because of its importance for waders such as redshank and lapwing. At one time the lapwing was a common sight on ploughed fields, but the use of insecticides and farming machinery has driven it to meadows and marshes in summer. Keep an eye open for the bright yellow ragwort, a plant that attracts the cinnabar moth, which lays its eggs on the stems and produces gaudy black-and-yellow caterpillars. In Freeman's Wood is a black poplar (*Populus nigra*), a native tree of lowland marshes and of this area, but not all that common. There are thought to be fewer than 3,000 black poplars in Britain today. The tree in Freeman's Wood is one of only two in Lancashire.

the ride

1 Begin from the large car park near the dock by crossing the road onto a cycleway along the edge of the **Lune Estuary**. A gravel track leads on to cross the River Conder before turning north through the **Conder Green car park**. (Follow the road right for The Stork pub.) Beyond the car park, ride onto a tree-lined track, and keep following this until it reaches a surfaced lane end, not far from the village of Aldcliffe.

2 Turn left into a **gravel area**, and then immediately, just before a footpath

stile, onto a broad vehicle track. At a cross-track, keep forward along a bridleway for **New Quay Road**, and going into **Freeman's Wood**. The track, now surfaced, crosses a section of **Aldcliffe Marsh**, and eventually comes out to meet a much wider road near a small light industrial complex. Keep forward until you reach an old arched bridge with the modern, **Millennium** (foot) **Bridge** near by.

3 Turn onto the footbridge, and then immediately right to leave it, without crossing the river. Go left on a surfaced **cycle lane** (signed for Halton and Caton). Follow the lane until it rises to run briefly alongside the main road. Almost immediately turn right to perform a loop to the left into an **underpass** – you may need to dismount here. On the other side, go forward on a **signed cycle route**, which passes beneath a bridge and goes forward on a surfaced track down an avenue of trees. When it forks, keep left, and carry on to reach the stone **Lune Aqueduct**. Just before it, turn right onto a narrow path that leads to the foot of a flight of steps. Here you will need to dismount and carry your cycle up the steps to reach the towpath – a breathless few minutes, but well worth the effort.

Looking across the Lune to Lancaster

2h30 — **14 MILES** — **22 KM** — **LEVEL 1**23

MAP: OS Explorer 296 Lancaster, Morecambe and Fleetwood

START/FINISH: Quayside, Glasson Dock; grid ref: SD446561

TRAILS/TRACKS: good route, though cyclists will need to dismount at a few points on the canal while passing waterfront pubs

LANDSCAPE: mainly old railway trackbed or canal towpaths

PUBLIC TOILETS: at the start

TOURIST INFORMATION: Lancaster, tel 01524 32878

CYCLE HIRE: none locally

THE PUB: The Stork, Conder Green

🛈 Cycles will need to be carried up and down steps to reach the canal towpath

Getting to the start

Glasson Dock is on the Lune Estuary, 4 miles (6.4km) south west of Lancaster. It is best reached from Lancaster, or Cockerham to the south, along the A588, but may also be reached from Junction 33 on the M6 via Galgate – turn left at the traffic lights in the village centre and follow signs.

Why do this cycle ride?

A superb introduction to coastal Lancashire. The old trackbed and the return along the Lancaster Canal makes for easy riding, while the traffic-free cycle route through riverside Lancaster is ingenious. You can opt out at the Millennium Bridge and explore Lancashire's ancient capital.

Researched and written by: Terry Marsh

4 Turn right along the towpath. At **Whitecross**, dismount again to change to the other side of the canal. At a couple of places now you may need to dismount again as you pass canalside pubs, but eventually a **bridge** leads back over the canal. Over the bridge, turn immediately right down steps (dismount again) to rejoin the **towpath**.

5 Continue until you pass **Bridge 95**, following which the canal has a road on the right, and bends to the left. A short way on, leave the towpath and go onto the road (near a **lodge** on the right, dated 1827). Go forward, climbing steadily into the village of **Aldcliffe**. At the top of the climb, on a bend, take care, and turn right into the first lane on the right, descending quite steeply, and continuing down past **houses**, to ride along a narrow country lane to rejoin the outward route near the gravel area.

6 Turn left onto the **trackbed**, and follow this back to Conder Green, turning left into the village for **The Stork**, or continue round the coast to **Glasson Dock**.

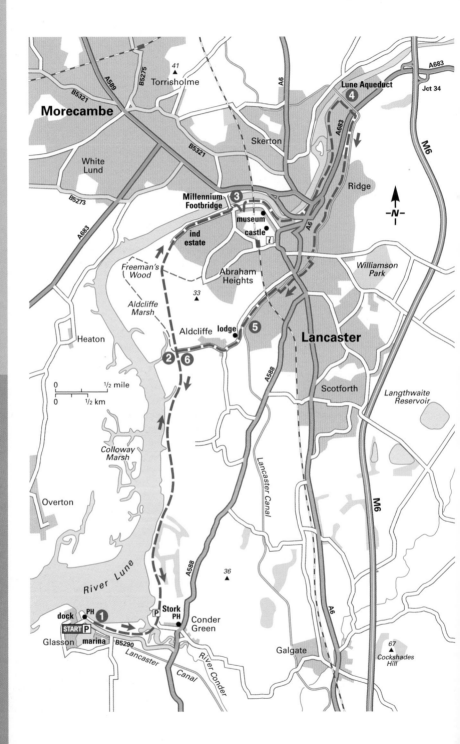

Lancaster **LANCASHIRE**

Morecambe

Torrisholme 41

Lune Aqueduct 4

Jct 34

White Lund

Skerton

B5273

Ridge

-N-

M6

Millennium Footbridge 3

museum

castle

ind estate

Freeman's Wood

Abraham Heights

Williamson Park

Aldcliffe Marsh 33

Aldcliffe lodge 5

Lancaster

Heaton

2 6

0   ½ mile
0   ½ km

Scotforth

Langthwaite Reservoir

Colloway Marsh

Lancaster Canal

M6

Overton

River Lune

A588

36

Scotforth

dock PH 1

Stork PH

Conder Green

START P marina

Glasson B5290

Lancaster Canal

River Conder

Galgate

67 Cockshades Hill

The Stork

about the pub

The Stork
Conder Green, Lancaster
Lancashire LA2 oAN
Tel: 01524 751234

DIRECTIONS: just off the A558 (west), a mile (1.6km) from Glasson and the start of the ride	
PARKING: 40	
OPEN: daily; all day	
FOOD: daily; all day Saturday & Sunday	
BREWERY/COMPANY: free house	
REAL ALE: Black Sheep Best, Timothy Taylor Landlord, Marston's Pedigree, guest beers	
ROOMS: 9 en suite	

A white-painted coaching inn spread along the banks of the estuary, where the River Conder joins the Lune estuary and just a short stroll along the Lancashire Coastal Way from the quaint seaport of Glasson Dock. The inn has a colourful 300-year history that includes several name changes. It's a friendly, bustling and ever-popular place, the draw being the location, the range of real ales, and the rambling, dark-panelled rooms, each with warming open fires. The south-facing terrace and patio look across the marshes.

Food
Seasonal specialities join home-cooked food such as steak pie, locally smoked haddock, salmon fillet with bonne femme sauce, and Lancashire sausage with onion gravy and mash.

Family facilities
Children of all ages are welcome and well catered for. There are family dining areas, family en suite accommodation, a children's menu, and a play area outside.

Alternative refreshment stops
There are plenty of cafés, restaurants and pubs in Lancaster.

☞ Where to go from here
A trip to Lancaster will be rewarded with a visit to the Maritime Museum, where the histories of the 18th-century transatlantic maritime trade of Lancaster, the Lancaster Canal and the fishing industry of Morecambe Bay are well illustrated (www.lancsmuseums.gov.uk). Take time to view Morecambe Bay or visit the Edwardian Butterfly House in Williamson Park (www.williamsonpark.com), or take a look at Lancaster Castle which dominates Castle Hill, above the River Lune. The Shire Hall contains a splendid display of heraldry (www.lancastercastle.com).

Lancaster

LANCASHIRE

Goosnargh and Beacon Fell Country Park

Ride the leafy lanes of Lancashire to the top of wooded Beacon Fell.

Sculpture Trail

From the Visitor Centre on Beacon Fell you can follow the Sculpture Trail featuring the work of local artist Thompson Dagnall, who uses materials found locally. Along the way you might find a serpent and, near the top of the fell, a bat hidden among the trees. All these are wooden, of course, but the country park is a remarkable habitat, and you should keep eyes and ears open for chaffinch, willow warbler, goldcrest, bullfinch, siskin and the occasional crossbill. Rabbits and hares are plentiful, too, and easily spotted in the bushes and the surrounding farm fields. Not surprisingly, they tend to be timid, as the sky here is patrolled by predatory kestrels, sparrowhawk and tawny owls on the lookout for a ready meal, and stoat, weasel and fox are not above a rabbit lunch.

The view from Beacon Fell across the Bowland Fells

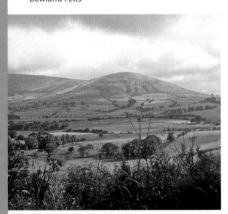

the ride

1 Begin past **Bushell House** and immediately turn left into **Mill Lane**, a narrow lane flanked by hedgerows, climbing gently. Continue past houses out into a more rural setting, and later descend through a dip to cross a bridge. Go past the end of **Broadith Lane**, and keep forward passing Curwen Lane, and remaining on Mill Lane to pass through a tunnel of trees to a crossroads.

2 Keep forward into **Syke House Lane**, with Beacon Fell soon coming into view. Stay on the main road, passing Church Lane and Bullsnape Lane, and, just after passing **Back Lane**, descend gently through bends into a dip and out through a lightly wooded stretch. Turn left for **Beacon Fell Country Park**, into Barns Lane.

3 When the road makes a pronounced right-hand bend, go left into **Carwags Lane**, leaving the main road for a very

Looking back towards Beacon Fell

3h00 **14 MILES** **22 KM** **LEVEL 123**

MAP: OS Explorer 286 Blackpool and Preston and OL41 Forest of Bowland and Ribblesdale

START/FINISH: Public parking adjacent to the church in Goosnargh; grid ref: SD559369

TRAILS/TRACKS: entirely on country lanes, some very narrow with high hedgerows

LANDSCAPE: rolling farmland

PUBLIC TOILETS: none on route

TOURIST INFORMATION: Clitheroe, tel: 01200 425566

CYCLE HIRE: Pedal Power, Waddington Road, Clitheroe, Lancashire BB7 2HJ, tel 01200 422066

THE PUB: Bushells Arms, Goosnargh

ⓘ There is a very long but steady ascent up to Beacon Fell and around its circular route, followed by equally long and steady descents

Goosnargh **LANCASHIRE**

narrow lane, and a very long and steady climb, which young children may find tiring, up towards Beacon Fell. On reaching, **Beacon Fell Road**, go forward into a one-way system.

4 At the turning to **Crombleholme Fold** you need to make a decision. The circuit around Beacon Fell is delightful, but one-way: Crombleholme Fold is the continuing route, but a short way beyond the junction lies the **Bowland Visitor Centre**, toilets, café and information point. Once you pass Crombleholme Fold, you are committed to cycling all the way around the fell, with still more ascent on the northern side. Cycling within the woodland is permitted, but only on surfaced tracks. If you go around the fell – recommended – you will be treated to lovely views northwards to the **Bowland Fells,** and in due course return to the Crombleholme Fold turning. Turn left, descending steeply. At a T-junction, turn left into **Bleasdale Road**, and shortly left again into **Button Street**.

Getting to the start
Goosnargh lies about 5 miles (8km) north east of Preston, and is easily reached via M6 (Jct 32) and M55 (Jct 1), north on A6 to Broughton, and then right to Goosnargh. At the post office, turn left into Church Lane, and follow this north to the start.

Why do this cycle ride?
Beacon Fell Country Park is an isolated hill rising to 873ft (266m), on the edge of the Bowland Fells. It is an area of rough moorland and woodland within the Forest of Bowland Area of Outstanding Natural Beauty, and was one of the first designated country parks in Britain. There are tremendous views north and south from the highest ground, and the approach along country lanes displays rural Lancashire at its very best.

Researched and written by: Terry Marsh

5 Follow a hedgerowed lane into the village of **Inglewhite**. Go past the village green to a crossroads, and keep forward into **Silk Mill Lane**, which gradually descends to cross **Sparting Brook**, climbing steadily on the other side. At a T-junction, turn right onto **Langley Lane** (signed for Preston).

6 Go through two S-bends, followed by a long, more or less straight and level section to a pronounced left bend (occasional flooding here), that leads down to a **hump bridge**, and a short climb beyond. Continue as far as **Goosnargh Lane**, and there turn left to return to **Goosnargh village**.

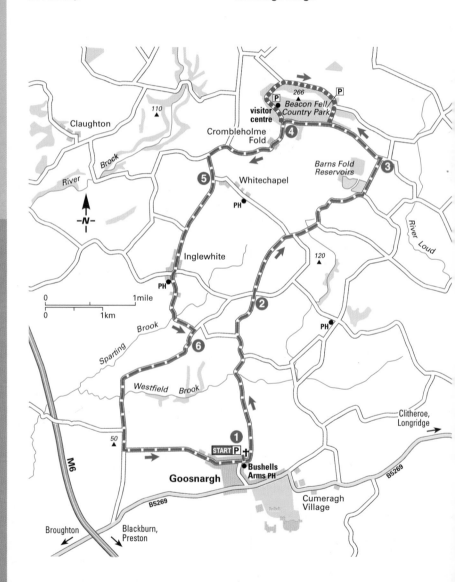

Goosnargh LANCASHIRE

Bushells Arms

Dr Bushell was a philanthropic Georgian who built his villagers not just a hospital, but this pub too. And he chose a lovely spot, beside the village green and overlooking the parish church. Expect a congenial and relaxing atmosphere in the cosy beamed bar, where you will find leather armchairs and a log fire in the stone fireplace. There's also an intimate, candlelit restaurant.

Food

For a light bite choose a few hot or cold dishes from the tapas menu, featuring items such as Greek salad, lamb in red wine and tomato sauce or calamari. For something more substantial order a range of tapas and mix and match your dishes.

Family facilities

Families are welcome and small portions from the tapas menu proove the ideal size for children. Make use of the secluded rear garden on fine days, replete with flower borders and a spacious lawn.

Alternative refreshment stops

Café, picnic and barbecue sites in the country park, plus pubs in Goosnargh.

☞ Where to go from here

Visit the ancient market town of Clitheroe and explore the town's 12th-century castle. The Castle Museum brings to life the history and geology of the Ribble Valley. At the National Football Museum in Preston you can take a fascinating trip through football past and present. There's a fine display of memorabilia, interactive displays that allow visitors to commentate on matches, and virtual trips to every League ground in the country (www.nationalfootballmuseum.com).

about the pub

Bushells Arms
Church Lane, Goosnargh
Preston, Lancashire PR3 2BH
Tel: 01772 865235

DIRECTIONS: see Getting to the start
PARKING: use public car park opposite
OPEN: daily
FOOD: daily; all day Sunday
BREWERY/COMPANY: Enterprise Inns
REAL ALE: Black Sheep Bitter, Tetley's Smooth, Boddington's

Cuerden Valley to Preston and back

Discover Chorley's best-kept secret, the valley of the River Lostock.

Flora & fauna

Most of Cuerden's 700 acres (284ha) are actively farmed, providing changing scenes throughout the year. The Valley Park is home to foxes, grey squirrels, great-spotted and green woodpeckers, patrolling buzzards and the occasional sparrowhawk, as well as a host of smaller birds, up to 70 species in all. The Preston Junction Nature Reserve, north of Bamber Bridge, is a good place to spot butterflies – common blue, small copper, meadow brown, wall brown,

gatekeeper, orange tip, small tortoiseshell. There are also some attractive ponds along this stretch, bright in spring and summer with yellow waterlilies. The reserve was built around the trackbed of the old Preston tramway.

Cuerden Hall is owned by the Sue Ryder Foundation and houses a small cafeteria; it is off-route, but easily accessible by turning left on reaching the A49 (rather than the route continuation, which goes right).

the ride

1 Leave the car park and immediately turn left onto the **Cuerden Valley Cycle Route**. At a junction bear left onto a slightly narrower track, and continue onto a surfaced track, climbing a little and then going forward to meet a main road. Turn right for 120 yards (100m), and then turn left to rejoin the cycle route.

2 The route through the valley park follows a broad, clear track, at one point bending right and left to pass through the edge of woodland before rejoining the course of the River Lostock to a bridge, water splash (for the adventurous) and **picnic tables**. Off to the right a short distance at this point is the **park lake**, which is home to numerous waterbirds, including at some times of year more than 250 Canada geese. Cross the bridge and go right, climbing briefly but steeply to follow a field edge path to a **bridge** spanning the M6 motorway, beyond which you descend to a car park and the A49.

3 Turn right on a **cycle lane** to a light-controlled crossing of the A6 at **Bamber**

Left: Cuerden Hall
Below left: Preston Junction Nature Reserve

2h30 · **13 MILES** · **20 KM** · **LEVEL 1**23

Bridge. Go forward, still on a cycle lane, as far as **Church Road**, and there cross the road at a safe crossing point, and turn into **Havelock Road**. Follow the road, shortly passing a small **industrial estate** to meet another lane. Turn right, and go past a **supermarket** car park, turning right onto a cycle lane once more, and through a low **tunnel** (dismount here). Just beyond, turn left beneath a road bridge into the edge of a housing estate. At a T-junction turn right towards a roundabout, but cross, left, just before it to enter the **Preston Junction Local Nature Reserve**.

4 Follow a clear track to a road. Cross and keep forward to cross another back lane. Go forward along the middle one of three possibilities. After a short rise the towers of **Preston** city centre come into view. Descend to cross over a farm access track, and keep on to meet a gravel track passing along the edge of **woodland**.

5 When the gravel track forks, branch right, descending to a track junction beside the **River Ribble**. Turn right to the next bridge, and here bear right and left to gain the bridge, across which the **Miller and Avenham Parks** mark the end of the route. Across the parks the centre of Preston is soon reached.

6 Return by re-crossing the bridge, but instead of dipping down to the Ribble, keep forward along an **avenue of trees** to meet the back lane crossed on the way out. Here rejoin the outward route, and retrace this first to **Bamber Bridge** and, once safely over the A6, back into **Cuerden Valley Park** and on to Whittle-le-Woods.

MAP: OS Explorer 286 Blackpool and Preston

START/FINISH: Whittle-le-Woods, Chorley, down Factory Lane; grid ref: SD575217

TRAILS/TRACKS: good tracks, stony in places, or surfaced

LANDSCAPE: river valley park, small urban section, woodland

PUBLIC TOILETS: none on route

TOURIST INFORMATION: Chorley, tel 01257 241693

CYCLE HIRE: none locally

THE PUB: Halfway House Hotel, Clayton-le-Woods

Getting to the start

Whittle-le-Woods is a suburb of Chorley, and lies along the A6, 2 miles (3.2km) north of the town. The start of the Cuerden Cycle Route is down Factory Lane in Whittle-le-Woods, just to the north of the church.

Why do this cycle ride?

Long stretches of traffic-free cycling through a wooded river valley are linked by safe cycling crossing points and cycle lanes into an old railway trackbed and then an even older tramway trackbed into city centre parks in Preston. The whole ride is through an intense area of habitat for a diverse range of flora and fauna. The ride can be shortened by taking a picnic as far as the bridge crossing in Cuerden Valley Park.

Researched and written by: Terry Marsh

Cuerden Valley

LANCASHIRE

Cuerden Valley LANCASHIRE

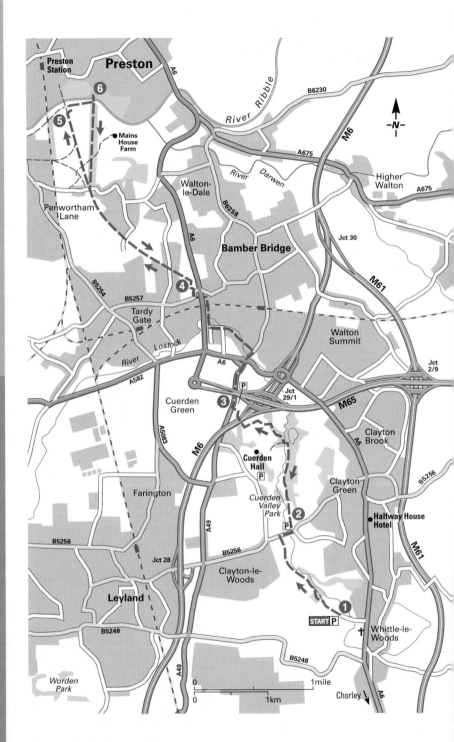

Preston Station

Preston

A6

River Ribble

B6230

M6

-N-

A675

Higher Walton

A675

Mains House Farm

River Darwen

Walton-le-Dale

B6258

Jct 30

Penwortham Lane

A6

Bamber Bridge

M61

B5254

B5257

Tardy Gate

River Lostock

Walton Summit

Jct 2/9

A582

A6

P

Jct 29/1

M65

Cuerden Green

A5003

3

M6

Cuerden Hall
P

Clayton Brook

A6

Faringdon

Cuerden Valley Park

Clayton Green

B5256

2
P

Halfway House Hotel

B5256

Jct 28

B5256

Clayton-le-Woods

M61

Leyland

A49

1

START P

B5248

Whittle-le-Woods

A49

B5248

Worden Park

0   1mile

0   1km

Chorley   A6

Halfway House Hotel

Reputedly at the exact 'halfway' point between London and Glasgow – hence its name – this modernised and comfortably refurbished roadside inn retains much of its former charm. It was once a favoured stopping point for charabancs bound for Blackpool and car travellers heading to and from Scotland. The traditionally furnished interior comprises a large lounge, dining room and a taproom with games area and the full range of Lees beers on tap. Note the lovely old sign on the gable entrance welcoming motorists and cyclists, a reminder of those early days of motoring and its time as a popular café for motorcyclists.

Food

Traditional pub food ranges from sausages and mash, pasta meals and lasagne to chargrilled pork chops and beef in black bean sauce. Sandwiches and light meals are also available.

Family facilities

Children can make good use of the outdoor play area in the beer garden on fine days. They are also welcome indoors and a children's menu is available.

Alternative refreshment stops

The ride passes near numerous restaurants, pubs and cafés in Preston and Chorley.

☛ Where to go from here

For a family fun outing that includes thrilling rides, jousting tournaments and spectacular magic shows, venture into King Arthur's Kingdom at Camelot Theme Park (www.camelotthemepark.co.uk) south of Leyland off the A49 near Charnock Richard.

about the pub

Halfway House Hotel
Preston Road, Clayton-le-Woods
Chorley, Lancashire PR6 7JB
Tel: 01772 334477

DIRECTIONS: beside the A6 a mile (1.6km) north of Factory Lane and the start of the ride

PARKING: 100

OPEN: daily; all day

FOOD: daily; all day

BREWERY/COMPANY: J W Lees Brewery

REAL ALE: J W Lees Bitter, Moonraker & seasonal beers

ROOMS: 36 en suite (adjoining Travelodge)

Astley Hall west of Chorley is a charming Tudor/Stuart building set in beautiful parkland and it manages to retain a 'lived in' atmosphere. There are pictures and pottery to see, as well as fine furniture and rare plasterwork ceilings (www.lancashiretourism.com).

Cuerden Valley

LANCASHIRE

Around Rivington and its reservoir

Explore Lever Park and discover Lord Leverhulme's ruined castle.

Castles and barns

Liverpool Castle is an intentional ruin, built on a small hill, Cob Lowe, by Lord Leverhulme as a replica of the castle in Liverpool Bay. It overlooks the waters of Lower Rivington Reservoir and has a fine view of Rivington Pike, one of Lancashire's best-known landmarks, one of a chain of beacon fires used to warn of danger. It was used at the time of the Spanish Armada in 1588.

Great House Barn is one of a small number of half-cruck barns in Lancashire, probably dating to Saxon times. Today it houses an information point, a gift shop

The calm waters of Rivington Reservoir

and tea room open every day of the year, except Christmas Day. Originally, it would have been used to shelter cattle and feed. From the barn an imposing driveway leads up to Rivington Hall, formerly the home of the Lord of the Manor. It has a fine red-brick Georgian façade, and, like the barns, was probably built on a site of Saxon importance.

the ride

1 Leave from the bottom end of the car park, passing a **barrier** and soon, at a track junction, turn left, descending to cross a narrow, **wooded gully**. Follow a clear track, around a field edge, to another track junction at the edge of large open area. Bear

right and follow a clear track to **Liverpool Castle**. From the castle entrance, head down a long woodland drive to meet a road.

2 Turn right for 330yds (300m), passing a **school**. At the end of **metal railings**, turn left up a surfaced lane to a rough stony track on the left, the lowest of three tracks at this junction. Follow this along an avenue of trees to another track junction, and there turn right, pass a **gate** onto a gently rising track. Continue forward at the next gate. When the track forks, bear left, and curve round left and right to a rough-surfaced lane beside **Rivington Hall**. Bear right to ride behind the hall into a car park.

3 Cross the car park, go forward past a wooden barrier and down a **stony driveway**, the right-hand of two exit drives. When the drive forks, bear right to a road. Emerge with care and turn right to pass **Rivington Stocks**, and going left with the main road. On reaching **Upper Rivington Reservoir**, leave the road by turning right onto a narrow road (bridleway).

Rivington Hall, built in the 18th century, is passed on the cycle route

1h30 — **7.5 MILES** — **12 KM** — **LEVEL 123**

MAP: OS Explorer 19 West Pennine Moors

START/FINISH: Great House Barn car park, Rivington; grid ref: SD628139

TRAILS/TRACKS: stony, woodland tracks and minor roads

LANDSCAPE: mainly woodland, some open areas around reservoirs

PUBLIC TOILETS: at start

TOURIST INFORMATION: Great House Barn (at the start)

CYCLE HIRE: none locally

THE PUB: The Millstone, Anderton

❶ Some short ascents, and one long road climb

Getting to the start

Great House Barn lies within Lever Park, on the edge of Horwich. Accessible from Junction 8 on the M61 motorway, and then along the A6 through Chorley to Adlington on the A673, or from Junction 6, and then by A6027 and through Horwich on the A673.

Why do this cycle ride?

The wild uplands and string of reservoirs of the West Pennine Moors make fine habitats for flora and fauna alike, and provide a network of tracks, paths and trails for exploring. Lever Park, sometime property of Lord Leverhulme, where this ride begins, has at its centre the attractive village of Rivington and historical buildings like the Great House Barn, Rivington Hall and Liverpool Castle.

Researched and written by: Terry Marsh

4 Continue beside the reservoir (left) and a large pond (right) to a gate on the left giving onto a stony track up to **Yarrow Reservoir**. Follow the track to a road at a gate.

5 Turn left, downhill, and follow the road left and across the reservoir road, passing **The Yew Tree Inn**. Go down a dip

and up the long, steady ascent of **Nickelton Brow** to a T-junction. Go left into New Road.

6 Turn left again at **Horrobin Lane**. Go down and cross between reservoirs, and then take the first turning on the right, rising through a small car park onto a **woodland track**. As this forks, keep ahead (right), and soon return to the start.

Rivington LANCASHIRE

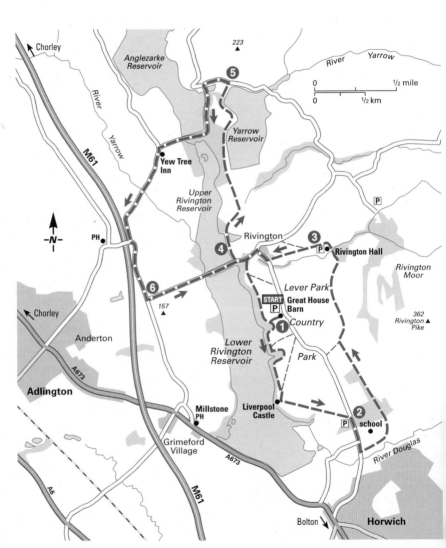

The Millstone

Occupying a glorious position overlooking Rivington Reservoir, the old Millstone pub has been stylishly converted into a contemporary bar-restaurant serving modern European food. Although, not really a 'pub' in the true sense of the word, you will find the atmosphere friendly and informal and the lunchtime menu light and good value. In addition, there's a splendid garden for summer eating and drinking, and it is a popular meeting place among local walking and cycling groups. It has a relaxing interior with wooden floors and wall panelling and a vibrant Mediterranean-style décor.

Food

Food is freshly prepared and takes in an imaginative range of eight pasta dishes among the lunchtime selection. Other dishes may include mustard and honey-glazed ham, roast lamb shank, and slow-roasted duck leg with citrus and spices.

about the pub

The Millstone
Bolton Road, Anderton
Chorley, Lancashire PR6 9HJ
Tel: 01257 480205
www.sanrocco.co.uk

DIRECTIONS: on the A673, 1 mile (1.6km) north west of Horwich. Turn right from the car park to the A673 at Horwich and turn right for the pub

PARKING: 80

OPEN: all day Saturday & Sunday; closed Monday except Bank Holidays

FOOD: daily; all day Sunday

BREWERY/COMPANY: free house

REAL ALE: none served

Family facilities
Children are very welcome here and smaller portions of all main meals are available.

Alternative refreshment stops
Picnic sites on the ride, the Yew Tree Inn and restaurants in Horwich and Anderton.

☞ Where to go from here
North of Chorley stands the Hoghton Tower, a fortified 16th-century house with a fascinating history. It was here in 1617 that the sirloin steak came into being, when King James I famously knighted a loin of beef. Cedar Farm Galleries at Mawdesley, 6 miles (9.7km) east of Chorley, offers contemporary crafts, unique shops, a café, farm animals and a funky playground (www.lancashiretourism.com).

Rivington LANCASHIRE

The Millstone

Occupying a glorious position overlooking Rivington Reservoir, the old Millstone pub has been stylishly converted into a contemporary bar-restaurant serving modern European food. Although, not really a 'pub' in the true sense of the word, you will find the atmosphere friendly and informal and the lunchtime menu light and good value. In addition, there's a splendid garden for summer eating and drinking, and it is a popular meeting place among local walking and cycling groups. It has a relaxing interior with wooden floors and wall panelling and a vibrant Mediterranean-style décor.

Food

Food is freshly prepared and takes in an imaginative range of eight pasta dishes among the lunchtime selection. Other dishes may include mustard and honey-glazed ham, roast lamb shank, and slow-roasted duck leg with citrus and spices.

about the pub

The Millstone
Bolton Road, Anderton
Chorley, Lancashire PR6 9HJ
Tel: 01257 480205
www.sanrocco.co.uk

DIRECTIONS: on the A673, 1 mile (1.6km) north west of Horwich. Turn right from the car park to the A673 at Horwich and turn right for the pub

PARKING: 80

OPEN: all day Saturday & Sunday; closed Monday except Bank Holidays

FOOD: daily; all day Sunday

BREWERY/COMPANY: free house

REAL ALE: none served

Family facilities

Children are very welcome here and smaller portions of all main meals are available.

Alternative refreshment stops

Picnic sites on the ride, the Yew Tree Inn and restaurants in Horwich and Anderton.

☛ Where to go from here

North of Chorley stands the Hoghton Tower, a fortified 16th-century house with a fascinating history. It was here in 1617 that the sirloin steak came into being, when King James I famously knighted a loin of beef. Cedar Farm Galleries at Mawdesley, 6 miles (9.7km) east of Chorley, offers contemporary crafts, unique shops, a café, farm animals and a funky playground (www.lancashiretourism.com).

Rivington **LANCASHIRE**

Haigh Country Park

Visit the seat of the Earls
of Balcarres and discover
the woodlands of Haigh.

Haigh Hall

You can't go in, but Haigh Hall was
previously the home of the Earl of Crawford
and Balcarres, and is a listed building dating
back to 1850. The nearby stable buildings
have been converted to a small museum,
café and gift shop, with a children's play
area near by. There's also a miniature
railway, which operates during the summer
months. Keep an eye open along the canal
for birdlife, especially kingfishers, which are

more common here than might be imagined.
Just on the edge of the estate, along
Copperas Lane, is a small pond. It was
formerly used for curling, and is known
as the 'Curling Pond'. Kingfishers love the
overhanging branches from which to feed.

the ride

1 Leave the car park and turn left (beware
speed ramps), and follow a hedgerowed
lane that soon starts to descend to a junction
with the B5239. This B-road is well used,
but there is a wide **footpath** on the right-
hand side, which can be used, if necessary,

to walk to the Leeds–Liverpool Canal.
Follow the road to **traffic lights** controlling
the narrow bridge spanning the canal.

2 Turn left onto the canal towpath at
the **Crawford Arms** pub, and follow the
towpath to an **iron trellis bridge** (No. 60) –
take care on the small humpback bridge
just before it. Here leave the towpath, and
carry bikes up a few steps to meet the main
estate road through Haigh.

3 Turn right, and after about 100 yards
(91m), turn right again on a broad
drive leading out to a gate, near a cottage,
at the top of **Hall Lane**. Ride down the lane
(rough in places, but motorable, and a
popular way into the woodlands of Haigh).
Approaching the River Douglas, Hall Lane
takes a wide sweep down to the **bridge**
spanning the river, from which it climbs
to meet the A49, at a T-junction.

4 Go left, and, if necessary, walk the
200 yards (182m) to the main Wigan
entrance to **Haigh Country Park**, passing
through ornate iron gates. Follow the broad,
descending track ahead, which soon crosses
the Douglas. Bear right, following the main
track as it curves around and begins the long,
steady climb back up to the **Leeds–Liverpool
Canal**, and then on to the straight drive
leading directly to the front of **Haigh Hall**.

5 Keep to the right of the Hall, and go up the
road behind it. **The Stables Centre**, café
and shop, are on the right. The car park is
directly ahead, just beyond the golf shop. Turn
left into the car park to complete the ride.

The golf course at Haigh Country Park

1h00 — **6 MILES** — **9.7 KM** — **LEVEL 1 2 3**

MAP: OS Explorer 276 Bolton, Wigan
and Warrington

START/FINISH: Haigh Country Park; grid ref:
SD596088

TRAILS/TRACKS: canal towpath, surfaced
estate or traffic roads. Stretch of 220yds
(200m) on a wide town road, which can be
walked. There are no cycle trails within Haigh
Country Park; cyclists are asked to use the
roads and trails with care for other users

LANDSCAPE: woodland, farmland and canal
towpath

PUBLIC TOILETS: Stables Centre, near start

TOURIST INFORMATION: Wigan Pier,
tel 01942 825677

CYCLE HIRE: none locally

THE PUB: Balcarres Arms, Haigh

❶ One long, steady climb. Beware speed
ramps on estate roads and care to be taken
alongside the canal

Getting to the start

Haigh Country Park is within easy reach
of both the M6 (Junction 27) and the M61
(Junction 6). From the M6, take the A49
towards Standish, then the B5239 to Haigh.
Look out for the B5239 and Aspull, then
Haigh, when leaving the M61. In Haigh, turn
down Copperas Lane, near the Balcarres
Arms, to reach the car park.

Why do this cycle ride?

Haigh Country Park has many attractions for
children and the woodlands have great
appeal plus almost 100 species of birds
during the year. The Leeds to Liverpool Canal
through the park provides an excellent
opportunity to explore.

Researched and written by: Terry Marsh

Haigh Country Park

LANCASHIRE

The sweeping driveway and symmetrical façade of Haigh Hall

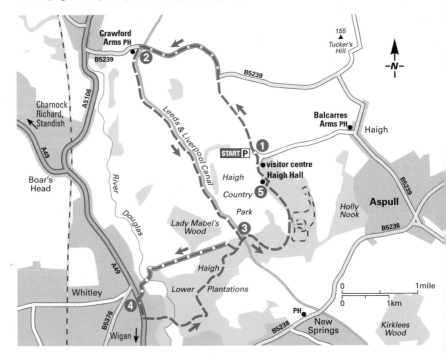

Balcarres Arms

Named after the Earl of Balcarres, who lived at nearby Haigh Hall, this is an unpretentious pub of some antiquity tucked away in historic Haigh, close to Haigh Country Park. Very much a locals' haunt, it is simply furnished and decorated and comprises a main bar and a cosy snug bar, and serves unfussy, home-cooked pub food.

Food
Expect light lunchtime bar snacks such as giant Yorkshires, baguettes and paninis alongside fish and chips and bangers and mash. A la carte choices iclude starters such as mushroom and Stilton bake and mains such as beef and ale pie, Viking gammon steak and vegetarian options.

about the pub

Balcarres Arms
1 Copperas Lane, Haigh
Wigan, Lancashire WN2 1PA
Tel: 01942 833377

DIRECTIONS: beside the Country Park access road in Haigh village, 0.5 mile (800m) from the start point of the ride
PARKING: 50
OPEN: daily; all day
FOOD: daily; no food Sunday to Tuesday evenings
BREWERY/COMPANY: free house
REAL ALE: Cocker Hoop, guest ales

Family facilities
Children are allowed inside and there's a standard children's menu for younger family members. Garden with picnic benches for summer alfresco drinking.

Alternative refreshment stops
The Stables café at the end of the route.

☞ Where to go from here
Head for Wigan Pier for a journey never to be forgotten. Part museum, part theatre, it is a mixture of entertainment and education. Step back in time at 'The Way We Were' heritage centre, visit Trencherfield Mill and the Machinery Hall, and then visit the Opie's Museum of Memories. There are also walks, talks, boat trips, events and much more.

Haigh Country Park

LANCASHIRE

91

Tatton Park to Dunham Park

Link two great estates –
Tatton and Dunham – and
get the best of both worlds.

A pub and two parks

It is always fascinating to research pub
names. They invariably tell a great deal
about the surrounding communities and
countryside. This route passes the Swan
with Two Nicks (corrupted in some parts of
England as the Swan with Two Necks, an
improbable likelihood). The name comes
from an association with the Vintners
Company, founded in 1357 by importers of
wine from Bordeaux. The company was
incorporated by Henry VI (1422–1461) into
one of the oldest of the Trade Guilds of
London. Its symbol is a swan with two nicks
on its beak. Then, as now, swans were the
exclusive property of the Crown, but a Royal
Gift was made to the Vintners, and each
year the Vintners would put a nick on each
side of the beak of cygnets to identify them
as Vintner's swans.

The ride also links two of Britain's old
estates, which offer a wealth of exploration
and learning for all ages.

Tatton Park: the Mansion and Tudor
Old Hall are set in 1,000 acres (405ha) of
beautiful rolling parkland with lakes, tree-
lined avenues and herds of deer. There are
award-winning gardens, a working farm, a
play area, speciality shops and a superb
programme of special events. There is
plenty here to entertain the family, but
there are extra charges for admission to the
mansion, garden, farm or Tudor Old Hall.

Dunham Park: An early Georgian house
built around a Tudor core, Dunham Massey
was reworked in the early 20th century, to
produce one of Britain's most sumptuous
Edwardian interiors. It houses collections
of 18th-century walnut furniture, paintings
and Huguenot silver, as well as extensive
servants' quarters. Here is one of the North
West's great plantsman's gardens with
richly planted borders and ancient trees, as
well as an orangery, Victorian bark-house
and well-house. The deer park contains
beautiful avenues and ponds and a Tudor
mill, originally used for grinding corn but
refitted as a sawmill c.1860 and now
restored to working order.

the ride

1 Leave the car park and ride out along
the driveway to the **Rostherne Entrance**
– keep an eye open for deer roaming in the
park. Cross the road onto the **Cheshire
Cycle Way West**, and ride on towards the
village of Rostherne. Just on entering the
village, turn left into **New Road**, climbing
steeply for a short while, and then
descending as it becomes **Cicely Mill Lane**,
and leads out to a junction of two A-roads,

The award-winning gardens in the grounds of Tatton Park

2h30 — **12.5 MILES** — **20 KM** — **LEVEL 1 2 3**

MAP: OS Explorer 267 Northwich and Delamere Forest and 276 Bolton, Wigan and Warrington

START/FINISH: Tatton Park (charge for admission); grid ref: SJ741815

TRAILS/TRACKS: Outside Tatton Park, the route is entirely on minor roads, with a major A-road crossing (at lights)

LANDSCAPE: Cheshire farmland and two major estate parks

PUBLIC TOILETS: at Tatton Hall

TOURIST INFORMATION: Knutsford, tel 01565 632611

CYCLE HIRE: none locally

THE PUB: Swan with Two Nicks, Little Bollington

🛑 Two major A-road crossings, one using traffic lights

Getting to the start
The main entrance is at Rostherne. You can take the A50 from Knutsford, then branch onto the A5034 and then on to a minor road (signed for Tatton Park).

Why do this cycle ride?
The opportunity to link two of Cheshire's important estates should not be missed. The ride follows quiet lanes across farmland landscape and reaches a mill and weir on the edge of Dunham Park. Both parks have family attractions. The nearby village of Rostherne is a lovely community of brick houses with a few thatched cottages.

Researched and written by: Terry Marsh

near the **Swan Hotel** at Bucklow Hill. The easiest thing to do here is dismount and cross the two roads (at traffic lights) as a pedestrian.

2 Cross into **Chapel Lane**, initially a long, straight road, leading to Hulseheath. Keep on, riding round bends, and then turn right into **Back Lane**. At a junction, go left into Thowler Lane, and at the next junction, bear right for Bollington, along **Boothbank Lane**.

3 On reaching **Booth Bank**, keep forward into **Reddy Lane** (signed for Bollington and Dunham Massey). Descend a little to pass beneath the M56 motorway, and then climbing around bends. The road eventually straightens and leads out to meet the A56, opposite a pub.

4 Cross the road with care, going left and then immediately right into **Park Lane**. Continue past the **Swan with Two Nicks** pub, to the end of the surfaced lane, where a narrow bridge crosses the **River Bollin**.

5 At **Bollington Mill**, go forward, but as the road bends left leave it by branching right onto a fenced and tree-lined path into **Dunham Park**.

6 Retrace the outward route. Avoid tempting alternative routes, as **Bucklow Hill** is the safest place to cross the Chester Road (A556).

The 18th-century Dunham Massey Hall

Tatton Park CHESHIRE

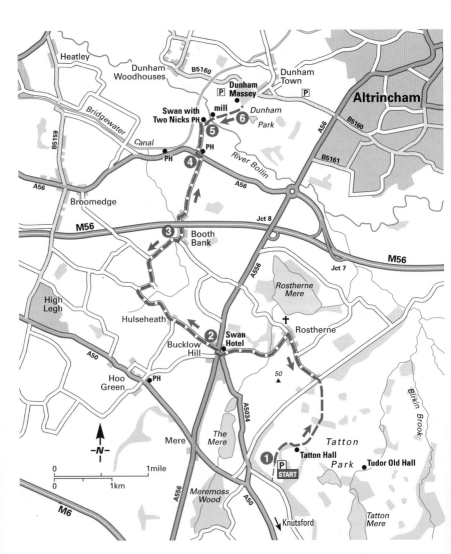

Swan with Two Nicks

Tucked away in a tiny hamlet close to Dunham Hall deer park, this distinctive, smartly refurbished pub is a real find and a super place for refreshments on this ride. Welcoming features include heavy ceiling beams, lovely antique settles, roaring winter log fires, while gleaming brass and copper artefacts and a wealth of bric-a-brac decorate the bars. There's also good seating in the patio garden, freshly prepared pub food, decent wines and three real ales on handpump.

Food

Typically, tuck into filled baguettes, jacket potatoes, various omelettes, sandwiches and salads at lunchtime, with main menu dishes including a hearty steak and ale pie, sausages and mash, grilled gammon and egg, and a range of pasta dishes. Specials are fish dishes such as pan-seared marlin with tomato and cucumber salsa.

Family facilities

A good welcome awaits families as children are allowed throughout the pub. There's a children's menu for youngsters.

Alternative refreshment stops

Stables Restaurant at Tatton Park serves hot meals, snacks and hot or cold drinks.

☛ Where to go from here

Take a closer look at Tatton Park, one of England's most complete historic estates (www.nationaltrust.org.uk), or visit nearby Tabley House, west of Knutsford, (www.tableyhouse.co.uk), the finest Palladian house in the North West, which holds the first great collection of English pictures ever made, and furniture by

about the pub

Swan with Two Nicks
Little Bollington, Altrincham
Cheshire WA14 4TJ
Tel: 0161 928 2914

DIRECTIONS: Little Bollington is signposted off the A56 between Lymm and the M56. The pub is in the village centre at the halfway point of the ride	
PARKING: 40	
OPEN: daily; all day	
FOOD: daily; all day Sunday	
BREWERY/COMPANY: free house	
REAL ALE: Timothy Taylor Landlord, Swan with Two Nicks Bitter, four guest ales	

Chippendale, Gillow and Bullock. Further afield is Jodrell Bank Visitor Centre (www.jb.man.ac.uk), where a pathway leads you 180 degrees around the massive Lovell radio telescope as it surveys the Universe. There's also an arboretum, and a 3-D theatre explores the solar system.

Tatton Park **CHESHIRE**

95

Middlewood Way

Leafy railway trackbed and canal towpath combine in this ancient transport circuit.

Poynton Coppice

Poynton Coppice is a fragment of ancient semi-natural woodland, and therefore a rarity. It has never been ploughed up or used for any purpose other than the production of timber. Only one-fifth of British woodland has this select status, and Poynton Coppice has not been disturbed since 1945, when the trees were cut off at ground level and left to grow back from the base. As a result, the wood contains trees that are all of the same age. In the coppice, you will find plants such as wood sorrel, woodruff and yellow archangel, all ancient woodland indicators, which by their presence demonstrate that the woodland has been established for a long time.

Coppicing used to be the most common form of woodland management, and relied upon the rotational cutting of regrowth to produce both underwood (the coppice) and large timber (standards). This not only provided medieval man with a continuous supply of wood in different sizes, but also produced woodland species with continuous woodland conditions in suitably different stages, particularly, a balance between light and shade.

the ride

1 Leave the car park by locating the path (near the play area) that leads up wide-spaced steps on the nearside of the viaduct to reach the **old railway trackbed**. You will need to carry or push bicycles up this short section. Once at the top, set off northwards along a delightful route, flanked by mixed woodland.

2h00	8 MILES	12.7 KM	LEVEL 1 2 3

MAP: OS Explorer 268 Wilmslow, Macclesfield and Congleton

START/FINISH: Adlington Road, Bollington; grid ref: SJ930780

TRAILS/TRACKS: old railway trackbed in good condition and canal towpath

LANDSCAPE: rural Cheshire, farmland rising to minor hills to the east

PUBLIC TOILETS: at the start and at Nelson Pit visitor centre

TOURIST INFORMATION: Macclesfield, tel 01625 504114

CYCLE HIRE: none locally

THE PUB: The Miners' Arms, Adlington

🛈 One steep downhill section, towpath is narrow in places with some seasonal overhanging vegetation. Steps to negotiate

Getting to the start
Bollington lies about 2.5 miles (4km) north east of Macclesfield. Leave the A523 for the B5090 and travel through the centre of Bollington. Look for signs to 'Middlewood Way', one of which directs you into Adlington Road. The car park, and an adjacent children's adventure play area, is about 200 yards (180m) down the road.

Why do this cycle ride?
This is a ride of contrasts. On the one hand, there is the pleasure of cycling along a renovated railway trackbed – the Middlewood Way – through light mixed woodland, and on the other, a delightful return along the towpath of the Macclesfield Canal, which has glorious views over the foothills of the Peak District National Park.

Researched and written by: Terry Marsh

Above: The Macclesfield Canal

2 **Poynton Coppice** is worth a brief detour on foot (see below). After that, as before, the on-going route description is easy, as the ride simply follows the trackbed as far as **Bridge 15**. Here, leave the trackbed, and go up (dismount here) to cross a minor road and reach the **Nelson Pit visitor centre**.

3 From the visitor centre, cycle up towards the car park, and there go through a narrow gap to join the towpath of the **Macclesfield Canal**. Turn right, and immediately cross a large, cobbled humpback bridge, and go beneath Bridge 15 to continue along the towpath. There are a couple of short sections between **Bridges 18 and 19** where the towpath dips briefly to the water's edge, and, with young children, it may be safer to dismount.

4 Leave the towpath at **Bridge 26**, by climbing up steps on the right to meet a minor road. Turn right, and follow the road as it drops very steeply to the northern edge of **Bollington,** and back to the Adlington Road car park.

Right: A sign made from a wheel on the Middlewood Way

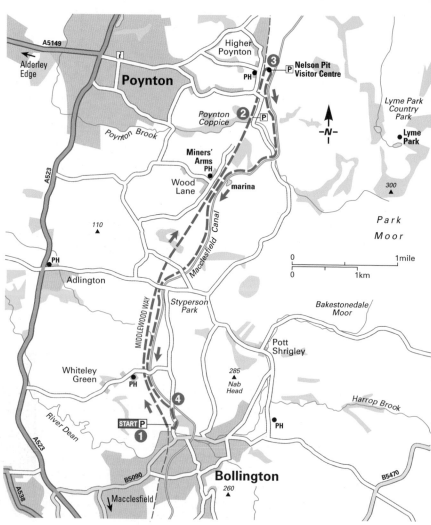

The Miners' Arms

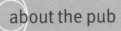

A big, bright and modern village pub that is well organised and set up to attract and entertain families. The spacious and airy bars and dining area are adorned with old farming memorabilia. Open fires add warmth and character to the place, and the friendly welcome to families extends to organising family fun days with children's entertainers. It is also popular with locals, walkers and cyclists, the latter having the use of bike racks in the car park.

Food
Traditional pub menus include a wide range of light meals, beef and ale pie, lamb shank, lasagne, oven bakes (lamb navarin and beef and beer casserole), and fish and chips.

Family facilities
In addition to the above, you'll find a children's menu, high chairs, family quiz nights, and a beer garden with a play area.

Alternative refreshment stops
Picnic sites along the Middlewood Way.

☛ Where to go from here
Magnificent Lyme Park, the largest house in Cheshire, has been the home of the Legh family for 600 years. It featured as Pemberley in the BBC's production of *Pride and Prejudice*. Visit the house and explore the gardens and 1,400 acre (567ha)

about the pub

The Miners' Arms
Wood Lane North, Adlington
Macclesfield, Cheshire SK10 4PF
Tel: 01625 872731
www.minersarms.info

DIRECTIONS: Wood Lane is located east off the A523 between Adlington and Poynton, just 150 yds (135m) off the cycle route

OPEN: daily; all day

FOOD: daily; all day

BREWERY/COMPANY: free house

REAL ALE: Theakston's, guest ales

park (www.nationaltrust.org.uk). Nether Alderley Mill near Alderley Edge dates from the 15th century and features original Elizabethan timberwork and Victorian machinery, and is in full working order.

Bollington CHESHIRE

Around Comberbach

An exploration of rural landscapes on quiet country lanes.

Willowherb

Stag heads are old trees, usually oak, with dead outer branches that resemble antlers. They are a common feature of the British countryside. Keep an eye open, too, for stands of great willowherb: this relative of the more common rosebay willowherb flourishes well along the country lanes of Cheshire and goes by a number of interesting names – cherry pie, apple pie and codlins-and-cream – across the country. 'Codlins' is an old, local name for cooking apples, and it is said that the flower and leaves of the great willowherb, when crushed, smell like apples, though it is a fragrance few can detect. The rosebay willowherb many regard as an invasive plant, but its ability to thrive on impoverished ground explains why it was the first plant to colonise the sites in London devastated during World War II. During Victorian times, however, it was often grown in gardens, and was by no means as widespread as it is now.

the ride

1 Ride out from the car park onto **Marbury Lane**, and at the main road, turn right. Take care on emerging at what is an awkward bend. Ride up to the village of **Comberbach** (pavement on the right, if needed). In the village turn left onto **Senna Lane**. Go past the post office and village stores (signed for Frandley). Beyond the last houses, the route runs along hedged lanes that lead to a junction. Bear right for Whitley, and keep going to the village of **Frandley**, there bearing left, and going forward into **Well Lane** (for Higher Whitley).

2h00 — 10.75 MILES — 17.2 KM — LEVEL 123

MAP: OS Explorer 267 Northwich and Delamere Forest

START/FINISH: Marbury Country Park (pay); grid ref: SJ653764

TRAILS/TRACKS: on roads throughout, mostly narrow, hedged country lanes used mainly by farm vehicles

LANDSCAPE: largely agricultural, with arable fields, hedgerows, trees and copses

PUBLIC TOILETS: none on route

TOURIST INFORMATION: Chester, tel 01244 402111

CYCLE HIRE: none locally

THE PUB: The Spinner & Bergamot Inn, Comberbach

❶ The start is along a moderately busy road, but with a pavement on one side, very short spell (33 yards/30m) on an A-road, with the option of walking on the footpath

Getting to the start

Comberbach lies 2.5 miles (4km) north west from Northwich, and Marbury Country Park between the two. The start is best reached from Northwich along the A533 to Anderton, and from the A559 along minor roads to Comberbach. The entrance to the country park is on a bend with poor visibility.

Why do this cycle ride?

The ride provides a splendid exploration of the Cheshire countryside, making use of hedged country lanes that network a wide spread of lush arable fields and isolated pockets of woodland that form part of the wider Mersey Forest. It also provides an end-of-ride opportunity to visit the Anderton Boat Lift, a unique feature along the canal ways of Britain.

2 Continue to a T-junction at the end of Well Lane, and turn right. Shortly, at the end of **Old Mill Lane**, at another T-junction, turn left into **Lake Lane**. The road immediately bends right. At the next T-junction, turn right in **Bentley's Farm Lane** (signed for Lower Stretton), and continue to reach the A559 at a crossroads near a pub.

3 Turn left along the A-road (dismount if necessary and use the footpath on the left) for a few yards, and then take the turning into **School Lane**, near the telephone box. Follow School Lane until you can turn left into **Booths Lane**, which, at a junction, joins Dark Lane. Keep left into **Dark Lane** and follow this into the village of Higher Whitley, which has an attractive duck-patrolled pond at its centre. Pass the pond, bearing left for Antrobus and Arley, and later turning right into **Normans Lane**. At the next junction, go right into **Old Mill Lane**.

Left: Farmland near Comberbach village
Top: Quiet country lane at Comberbach

Researched and written by: Terry Marsh

4 At the end of the lane, turn left into **Goosebrook Lane**, which soon climbs gently before levelling and descending gently. At the far end of the lane, at a Y-junction, turn right into **Hall Lane**, and keep on to the next T-junction, there going left for Comberbach.

5 At the next junction turn right into **Hough Lane** (signed for Barnton),

and follow the lane, climbing gently. At the next junction, branch left, still in Hough Lane, finally leaving Hough Lane at the next junction, by going forward onto **Cogshall Lane**. Follow the lane to a T-junction with a main road. Turn left and soon go steeply downhill (pavement on the right), through a dip and up the other side to the turning into the **Marbury Country Park**.

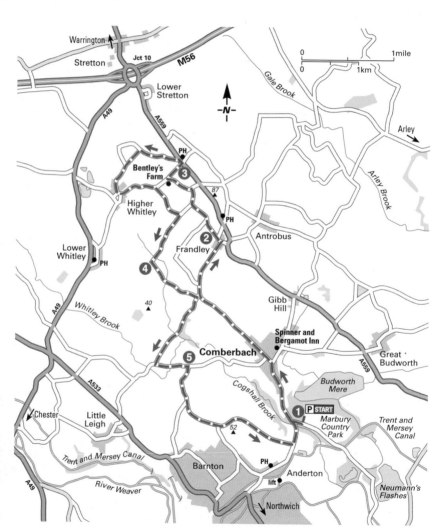

The Spinner & Bergamot Inn

Formerly called the Spinner, and built by local landed gentry, allegedly for 'private rendezvous' with mistresses, today the pub crams simple charm into its warren of small rooms decorated with Toby jugs and horse brasses. Crackling log fires add warmth and cheery welcome on cold winter days. Outside, summer seating is available on a terrace, which overlooks a Crown bowling green.

Food

Food is freshly prepared using local produce, including bread from the village baker. Typically, the menu may offer Bury black pudding for starters followed by medley of butcher's sausages with mash and onion gravy, or liver and onions.

Family facilities

Children are welcome in the bars. There's no children's menu but smaller portions of many of the main dishes are available.

Alternative refreshment stops

Picnic tables throughout Marbury Country Park plus a barbecue site.

☛ Where to go from here

Take a trip to remember on the world's first boat lift. Experience the fully restored and re-opened Anderton Boat lift and watch the lift operators at work (www.andertonboatlift.co.uk). Children aged between 2 and 13 will love Gullivers World Theme Park at Warrington

about the pub

The Spinner & Bergamot Inn

Warrington Road, Comberbach
Northwich, Cheshire CW9 6AY
Tel: 01606 891307

DIRECTIONS: at the junction with Budworth Lane in the centre of Comberbach, a mile (1.6km) from Marbury Country Park	
PARKING: 110	
OPEN: daily; all day	
FOOD: daily; all day Sunday	
BREWERY/COMPANY: Punch Taverns	
REAL ALE: Greene King IPA & Old Speckled Hen, Theakston's Black Sheep	

(www.gulliversfun.co.uk/warrington.htm). Don't miss Walton Hall Gardens (www.warrington.gov.uk/entertainment /parks/walton.htm).

Willaston to Parkgate

Start from an old railway
station and follow the
Wirral Way to a seafront
resort with no sea.

Parkgate

Parkgate is unique in the North West; it
looks very much like a traditional Victorian
seaside resort with terraced houses, shops
and hotels. Once the seafront gave onto
golden sands, but the sea abandoned
Parkgate more than 50 years ago, leaving
the sands to revegetate into the grassy
marshes you see today. The encroaching
marsh finally reached the sea wall along
The Parade at the end of World War II.

To the south of Parkgate, you can still find
what remains of the Old Quay, evidence of
the flourishing 16th century, now wholly
landlocked. It is hard to believe that once
the water here was deep, and provided a
safe anchorage.

Where the trackbed runs through the
rock cutting, note the grooves made by the
railway engineers as they cut through the
sandstone bedrock. On one side, a lower
wall and small sandstone cliffs are covered
with mosses and ferns that love this kind of
sheltered, moist environment.

the ride

1 Set off by riding to the far end of the
car park and turning right through a

1h30 — **7.5 MILES** — **12 KM** — **LEVEL 1**23

MAP: OS Explorer 266 Wirral and Chester

START/FINISH: Hadlow Road railway station, Willaston; grid ref: SJ332774

TRAILS/TRACKS: former railway trackbed, rough-surfaced and muddy in a few places, but generally in good condition. Short section of road, in Parkgate, which can be avoided by stopping before reaching it and returning from there

LANDSCAPE: mainly farmland, with light woodland along the old trackbed

PUBLIC TOILETS: at the start (in Ticket Office) and at Parkgate

TOURIST INFORMATION: Birkenhead, tel 0151 647 6780; www.visitwirral.com

CYCLE HIRE: none locally

THE PUB: The Nag's Head, Willaston

Parkgate **CHESHIRE**

Getting to the start

The village of Willaston lies between Neston and Ellesmere Port, and is best reached from the A540, along the B5151, or from the M53 (Junction 6) along the B5133. The car park is at the former Hadlow railway station, just at the southern edge of the village.

Why do this cycle ride?

Tree-lined tracks, picturesque villages, an authentic railway station complete with ticket office, views of the Dee Estuary and the Welsh hills, rock cuttings and a wealth of wildlife – and delicious home-made ice cream available in Parkgate.

Researched and written by: Terry Marsh

Shaded view across fields at Willaston

narrow gap to gain the **Wirral Way cycle track**, which immediately passes the station platform, before reaching a gate. Cross the road with care, and continue on the other side, riding through lush arable farmland, along a fine corridor of trees and shrubs.

2 For a while after a **stone bridge**, the track becomes a little more rough, and runs on to a gate immediately before a road underpass. Go through the **underpass** and on the other side, pass through another gate to resume the Wirral Way. Eventually the track continues to run through a **railway cutting**, with steep sides and overhanging vegetation.

Railway station museum at Willaston, recalling early 20th-century rail travel

Optional Extension

Extend the ride a little by emerging with care onto the road, and riding to the right for just over 100 yards (90m), and, as the road bends to the right, leave it by branching left onto a continuation into **light woodland** of the Wirral Way.

Keep going as far as a bridge where the cycle route circles right and passes beneath the bridge, to go forward along an estate road leading down into Parkgate. At **The Parade** (the seafront), turn left. This is always busy, and it may be safer if parties with young children dismount and walk to the far end of **Parkgate**. Either way, press on to the southern end of Parkgate and turn left as the road now climbs steadily to return to Point 4 above. Turn right, back onto the original route and retrace the outward ride.

3 When the track emerges at a road (Mellock Lane) keep forward into **Station Road**, and cycle down to pass beneath a railway line and reach a small car park. Ride past this and resume the **Wirral Way**. Continue until the cycle route emerges near a car park, beyond which a broad track leads down to a main road on the edge of **Parkgate**.

4 Return from this point, back the way you came.

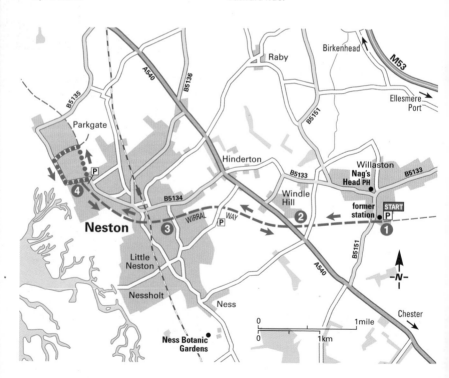

The Nag's Head

Built in 1733 and tucked away in the old part of Willaston, The Nag's Head is a welcoming pub to retreat to after the ride, with cushioned settles, comfy chairs and open log fires in the relaxing bars. In the summer, the alfresco decking terrace with big benches and umbrellas provides a convivial setting for outdoor eating and drinking.

Food

Expect a straightforward pub menu offering snacks – ploughman's lunches and sandwiches – and main meals such as broccoli and cream-cheese bake, home-made steak and kidney pie, and curries. Some gluten-free dishes are also available.

Family facilities

There's a genuine welcome here for families and young children have their own menu.

Parkgate CHESHIRE

about the pub

The Nag's Head
Hooton Road, Willaston
Cheshire CH64 1SJ
Tel: 0151 327 2439

DIRECTIONS: in Willaston village centre on the B5133. Within walking distance of Hadlow Road Station

PARKING: 40

OPEN: daily; all day

FOOD: daily; all day until early evening

BREWERY/COMPANY: Enterprise Inns

REAL ALE: changing guest ales

Alternative refreshment stops

Pollards in Willaston and the Ship and the Red Lion on the Parade in Parkgate.

☞ Where to go from here

Discover how canals shaped Britain's heritage and see the world's largest collection of canal craft in a 200-year-old dock complex at the Boat Museum in Ellesmere Port (www.boatmuseum.org.uk). Ness Botanic Gardens overlooking the Dee estuary offers all round interest (www.nessgardens.org.uk), while the Blue Planet Aquarium near Ellesmere Port features two floors of interactive displays and an underwater moving walkway that takes you on a journey through the waters of the world. View huge sharks, deadly poisonous frogs and over 2,500 fish (www.blueplanetaquarium.com).

Around Willington, Utkinton and Kelsall

Willington CHESHIRE

Vistas of the lush Cheshire countryside.

Deer sheltering from the bright sunshine under a tree in a field at Willington

Fruity traditions

The village of Willington has a long tradition of fruit growing, so keep an eye open for fields of rhubarb or strawberries, as well as apple orchards and wild damson trees in the hedgerows. Damsons, normally associated with pies and jams, were also used to provide a dye for clothing and to add to whitewash to create pastel colours for room decoration. You may also spot some deer in a large park beside the route.

1h30 — **7 MILES** — **11 KM** — **LEVEL 123**

MAP: OS Explorer 267 Northwich and Delamere Forest

START/FINISH: Chapel Lane, Willington; grid ref: SJ531667

TRAILS/TRACKS: entirely on quiet country lanes, but with numerous ascents and descents

LANDSCAPE: mainly farmland

PUBLIC TOILETS: none on route

TOURIST INFORMATION: Chester, tel 01244 402111

CYCLE HIRE: Eureka Cyclists Cycle Hire, Woodbank, Chester, tel 0151 339 5629; www.eurekacyclists.co.uk

THE PUB: The Boot Inn, Boothsdale

🛈 Although fairly short this is an undulating ride on twisting and sometimes steep narrow lanes. Good road sense required

Getting to the start

Willington is one of many small villages in this part of rural Cheshire. The easiest approach is along the A54 Winsford to Tarvin road, or along the A556 from Northwich. An alternative is to head for Kelsall, and then by rural lanes to Willington. There is a small car park in Chapel Lane.

Why do this cycle ride?

This is a splendid exploration of pastoral Cheshire, following undulating and twisting lanes – care needed at all times against approaching traffic – and linking three charming villages. Cameo vistas of the lush Cheshire countryside come and go, seen through hedgerow gaps and from the top of country lanes.

Researched and written by: Terry Marsh

Willington CHESHIRE

the ride

1 Leave the parking area in Chapel Lane and go left to **Willington Road,** turn left again. Follow the lane as it bends through a dip, and climbs gently flanked by hedgerows and woodland. At **Willington Hall Hotel,** turn left on a side road for **Utkinton,** climbing steeply. Soon you start to pass through **farmland**, bound for the village of Utkinton.

2 On reaching Utkinton, turn left into **Quarrybank**, now tackling a long, steep climb with good views on the right to distract from the effort. At the top of the climb, at the entrance to **Rowley Farm**, the road swings left. Keep following Quarrybank, still climbing, now more easily, and then beginning a long descent.

3 At a T-junction, go left, signed for **Kelsall**. Pass along the edge of **Primrosehill Wood**, a detachment from Delamere Forest mainly of Scots and Corsican pine, and continue towards Kelsall, before breaking out into farmland once more. Continue past the **Summer Trees Tea Shop**, and then take the next turning on the right into **Waste Lane**. A long,

steady descent leads round a bend, and then go forward to the edge of Kelsall. At a crossroads, turn left, by **Th'ouse at Top pub**, and follow the road round towards the centre of Kelsall.

4 Opposite the church, as the road bends to the right, turn left into **Church Street**. The road now descends to a T-junction. Go left into **Common Lane**, and then take the next left, signed for Willington and Utkinton. Now climb once more, past **farms** and large houses.

5 At the next junction turn right, for **Utkinton**. Go through a dip, passing the turning to **The Boot Inn**, and keep forward to complete the ride at Chapel Lane.

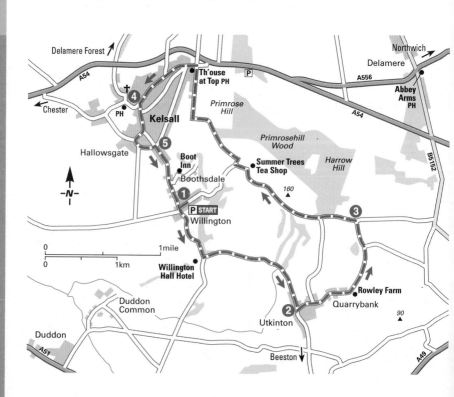

The Boot Inn

A real hidden gem in a superb setting on a wooded hillside, with views across the Cheshire plain to the Cllwydian hill, this quiet dining pub, originally a small ale house, has been converted from a charming row of sandstone cottages. Inside, it has been opened up, but you will find quarry-tiled floors, old beams, crackling log fires, and plenty of cosy alcoves around the central bar. An extension with French windows overlooks the small, sun-trap garden. The Boot offers tip-top ales – try the local Weetwood brews – decent wines and freshly prepared food.

Food

You're spoiled for choice if you fancy a hearty snack, as there are home-made soups with crusty bread, hot paninis, sandwiches (beef and horseradish), salad platters and hot baguettes filled with pork and peppers with hoisin sauce. Main meals take in braised shoulder of lamb with root vegetables and red wine, breast of duck with orange and cranberry, and smoked haddock with rarebit topping.

Family facilities

Although there are no special facilities for children, there is a family dining area and smaller portions of the main menu dishes can be ordered.

Alternative refreshment stop

Summer Trees Tea Shop on the route. Pubs and restaurants in Kelsall.

☞ Where to go from here

Children will enjoy a visit to Chester Zoo, the largest zoological gardens in Britain, with 7,000 animals and 500 species. Look for the penguin pool, the Bat Cave for endangered bat species, the National Elephant Centre, and the children's Fun Ark (www.chesterzoo.org). At Beeston Castle there are 4,000 years of history to be discovered and breathtaking views from the Pennines to the mountains of Wales (www.english-heritage.org.uk).

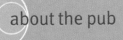

about the pub

The Boot Inn

Boothsdale, Willington
Tarporley, Cheshire CW6 0NH
Tel: 01829 751375

DIRECTIONS: signposted left off the minor road south of Kelsall towards Willington. Near the end of the cycle ride

PARKING: 60

OPEN: daily; all day Friday, Saturday & Sunday

FOOD: daily; all day Saturday & Sunday

BREWERY/COMPANY: free house

REAL ALE: Greene King Pedigree, local Wheetwood ales, Bass

Willington CHESHIRE

Acknowledgements

The Automobile Association would like to thank the following photographers, companies and picture libraries for their assistance in the preparation of this book.

Abbreviations for the picture credits are as follows: - (t) top; (b) bottom; (l) left; (r) right; (AA) AA World Travel Library.

Front cover AA/J Sparks; Back cover AA/T Mackie; 1 AA/J Sparks; 6/7 AA/J Sparks; 12 AA/J Sparks; 13 AA/J Sparks; 15 AA/J Sparks; 16 AA/J Sparks; 17 AA/J Sparks; 19 AA/J Sparks; 20bl AA/J Sparks; 20/21 AA/J Sparks; 23tl AA/J Sparks; 23br AA/J Sparks; 24/25 AA/T Marsh; 27 AA; 28bl AA/J Sparks; 28/29t AA/J Sparks; 31 AA/J Sparks; 32 AA/S Day; 35 AA/E A Bowness; 36 AA/J Sparks; 37 AA/J Sparks; 39 AA/J Sparks; 41 AA/J Sparks; 42 AA/J Sparks; 43 AA/R Ireland; 44 AA/E A Bowness; 45 AA/E A Bowness; 47 AA; 48 AA/J Sparks; 51tl AA/J Sparks; 51br AA/E A Bowness; 52/53 AA/T Marsh; 54 AA/S Day; 55 Sawrey Hotel, Far Sawrey; 57 AA/J Sparks; 58 AA/T Marsh; 59 AA/E A Bowness; 60bl AA/J Sparks; 60/61 AA/J Sparks; 63 AA/E A Bowness; 64 AA/J Sparks; 65 AA/J Sparks; 67 AA/J Sparks; 68 AA/E A Bowness; 70 AA/E A Bowness; 71 Cavendish Arms, Cartmel; 72/73 AA/T Marsh; 75 AA/T Marsh; 76bl AA/T Marsh; 76/77 AA/T Marsh; 79 AA/T Marsh; 80 AA/T Marsh; 81 AA/T Marsh; 83 AA/T Marsh; 84 AA/D Forss; 85 AA/D Forss; 87 AA/T Marsh; 88 AA/T Marsh; 90 AA/T Marsh; 91 AA/T Marsh; 92/93 AA/S Day; 94 AA/S Day; 95 AA/T Marsh; 96/97 AA/T Marsh; 98 AA/T Marsh; 99 AA/T Marsh; 100 AA/T Marsh; 101 AA/T Marsh; 103 AA/T Marsh; 104/105 AA/T Marsh; 106 AA/T Marsh; 107 AA/T Marsh; 108/109 AA/T Marsh; 111 AA/T Marsh

Every effort has been made to trace the copyright holders, and we apologise in advance for any accidental errors. We would be happy to apply the corrections in the following edition of this publication.